Judge Me Please

Gary D. Strunk

TEACH Services, Inc.

P U B L I S H I N G

www.TEACHServices.com

Copyright © 2012 TEACH Services, Inc.
ISBN-13: 978-1-57258-743-4 (Paperback)
ISBN-13: 978-1-57258-744-1 (Hardback)
ISBN-13: 978-1-57258-745-8 (ePub)
ISBN-13: 978-1-57258-751-9 (Kindle)
Library of Congress Control Number: 2011944165

Published by
TEACH Services, Inc.
P U B L I S H I N G
www.TEACHServices.com

Table of Contents

Preface

It troubles me that I know of Adventist ministers who are leaving the Adventist faith because they profess to have lost confidence in our sanctuary doctrine and its related doctrine of the investigative or pre-advent judgment. Some have even gone so far as to say, "Nothing happened in 1844." My impression is that they lost faith in a doctrine about which they had limited knowledge and could not answer questions raised by others. Most Adventists have read that in 1844 Christ moved from the holy place to the Most Holy Place of the heavenly sanctuary to begin the investigative judgment, which involves examining the records of those who have professed faith in God to determine who will go to heaven and who will not. Most people know little beyond that.

The investigative judgment and review of the records is not to improve God's knowledge. He already knows. It is to prove the fairness of God to the angels and beings of the unfallen worlds. Unless a person has also rejected the very clear teaching of the state of the dead and the visible return of Christ, it should be clear that when Jesus returns He will resurrect the righteous dead, translate the living righteous, strike dead the living wicked, and leave the wicked dead in the graves. Therefore a pre-advent judgment of some kind must take place before Jesus returns.

I entered this study with complete confidence in the Bible and the Spirit of Prophecy, which is a good attitude to have when seeking for greater light from those sources. That confidence is based upon *many* evidences for faith other than the topic of the judgment. For years I have been impressed with the accuracy of our pioneers' Bible knowledge. They didn't have it all, but what they had was far superior to their Protestant counterparts. God truly led them. But there is more, and it is my hope that this study of the judgment will help us uncover the more and, if nothing else, will stimulate further investigation of the subject that desperately needs to be illuminated to settle us deeper into the faith. Ellen White wrote:

> The great plan of redemption, as revealed in the closing work for these last days, should receive close examination. The scenes connected with the sanctuary above should make such an impression upon the minds and hearts of all that they may be able to impress others. All need to become more intelligent in regard to the work of the atonement, which is going on in the sanctuary above. When this grand truth is seen and understood, those who hold it will work in harmony with Christ to prepare a people to stand in the great day of God, and their efforts will be successful (*Testimonies for the Church*, vol. 5, p. 575).

Ellen White points us to the importance of personal Bible study, as she herself wrote, "The written testimonies are not to give new light, but to impress vividly upon the heart the truths of inspiration already revealed" (*Testimonies for the Church,* vol. 5, p. 665). When our pioneers did not understand a text or passage, or had the wrong interpretation of a text or passage, she was often silent. Some areas of truth were only partially understood in her day. Her writings carry us only a little way beyond the understanding of our pioneers, so that it is left for us to study those topics further, leaving them open to our investigation. And what a rich treasure is ours if we dig, ask the right questions, and trust that what is already in our hands is not fool's gold but is the genuine item—gold refined in the fire that we may be rich, and that we may secure white raiment that we may be clothed.

I am not always satisfied with the *what* of a subject. I want to know the *whys*. I think this can be seen beginning in chapter 3. I am trying to understand the whys of the investigative judgment where our richer treasure awaits. There may be better whys than I have suggested, but the ones I have shared here are my thoughts at this time.

Chapter 1

When You Don't Feel Righteous

Once upon a time there was a little boy who learned to steal, cheat, lie, and disobey. His grandmother kept her purse in the pantry just off the kitchen. While presumably puttering around, he would go into the pantry, open his grandmother's purse, and take out dimes, quarters, and nickels. As he would emerge from the pantry, he would smile sweetly at his grandmother and go outside to play. If his grandmother suspected any misconduct, she did him no favor by not stopping him. Soon it spread outside the home. He would steal candy, trinkets to wear on his belt, and anything he thought he needed from the stores in town. Soon he had a price on his head for "whoever was stealing from the stores." To steal, to lie, or cheat was a way of life.

But it was taking its toll. If he simply *thought* of doing something wrong, he would spin out an alibi that would take him from point A to point B to point C and beyond, until finally he would shake himself to realize he hadn't done anything yet. No one suspected him really. On his way to school, he might pick some flowers from a neighbor's yard to give to the teacher. He was such a nice boy!

But it made him feel guilty and fearful. If he saw a police car, he would hide behind a tree or dart down the alley just in case. At every accusation he felt guilty. If the teacher asked the class, "Has anyone seen my ruler?" He thought she was accusing him. If the kids behind him were whispering and laughing, he thought they were laughing at him.

Little did he know he was developing an untrustworthy conscience, an oversensitive conscience from continually resisting his conscience.

In time he became a Christian, but his evil imagination didn't stop. Years of practice had etched deep brain nerve pathways that were still active. So, while listening to sermons, he felt guilty. Guilty! Guilty! In time, he was afraid to pray. Then he had no desire to pray. He was doing his best but feeling guilty. He was like David, "I acknowledge my transgressions, and my sin is always before me" (Ps. 51:3). He couldn't make himself forget the past. Even though he was not doing any of the things he used to do, the past haunted him, and the possibility of doing them again rose up before him continually. More guilt … until several years later when a truth settled in from 1 John.

> My children, let us love not merely in theory or in words—let us love in sincerity and in practice! If we live like this, we shall know that we are children of the truth and can reassure ourselves in the sight of God, even if our own hearts make us feel guilty. For God is infinitely greater than our hearts, and he knows every-thing. And if, dear friend of mine, when we realise this our hearts no longer accuse us, we may have the utmost confidence in God's pres-

ence. We receive whatever we ask for, because we are obeying his orders and following his plans (1 John 3:18-21, Phillips).

This is how we may know that we belong to the realm of truth, and convince ourselves in his sight that even if our conscience condemns us, God is greater than our conscience and knows all (1 John 3:19, 20, NEB).

By genuinely loving our brother we may know that we are children of the truth, or of God. This knowledge will enable us to stand confidently in the presence of God, for even though our heart condemns us, since we are still sinners, we know that God is greater than our heart, His knowledge and understanding far surpass our own, and He is able to perceive our sincerity and to allow for the mistakes into which we fall (1 John 3:19, 20, paraphrased, *SDA Bible Commentary*, vol. 7).

What a precious passage! Precious truth! Precious God! Even allowing us to slip without condemning. Is there a way to believe we are accounted righteous and treated as if we were righteous even when we don't feel righteous? Is this a part of righteousness by faith everyone talks about? Because all sinners face temptations and some guilt that they must deal with.

Guilt can make us misread God. Paul Heubach told the story many times of a woman who came into the pastor's office ... and sat there, and sat there. Finally she spoke. "I can't please God." Then she sat there some more. "I can't please God. I've tried and I've tried, and I can't please God."

The pastor patiently asked her about her upbringing, trying to figure out where these feelings were coming from. Her story began to unfold. When she was a little girl, her daddy died. Her mommy had to find a job, working long hours each day. Each day she came home tired, disappointed, and angry. She would pick on the little girl and criticize her and scold her and hurt her. Neither she nor the girl realized at the time the damage being done to the little one. To this little girl, her mommy was still queen in her eyes, as every child wants of their parents.

One day it was her mother's birthday. The little girl wanted to surprise her mommy when she came home. She busied herself all afternoon in the kitchen, preparing supper to have it just right when Mommy arrived. She timed everything like a master chef. She even baked her mother's favorite biscuits. It was going to be a big surprise for Mommy. And just as Mommy came through the door, she placed the biscuits on the table and stepped back with a big smile on her face.

But when her mommy came into the kitchen and looked around, her first words were, "Such a mess! Haven't I told you when you work in this kitchen …" And on and on she ranted until that little girl's heart was crushed. And now, thirty years later, she was saying, "I've tried and I've tried, and I can't please God."

Sometimes we have to spend a lot of time *unlearning* what we think we know about God, since parents stand in the place of God when we are children. And as children we can poison our own minds through misbehavior that leads us to misread God and all the precious truths awaiting us.

When the beloved, aged, well-experienced John wrote, "If we confess our sins, He is faithful … to forgive us our sins" (1 John 1:9), he knew His Lord well—he knew how truly faithful He is! He will forgive! When we plead for forgiveness, we are not trying to overcome a reluctant God. He wants to forgive. He wants to restore and cleanse us from all unrighteousness.

It's hard to look objectively at the fruit of the Spirit in ourselves. We may *know* that we are changed, that God has given us a new heart with all the love for our brethren, and that we want to live for God, to please God. But the baggage of condemnation and guilt of the past crowds out the assurance that God wants to give us.

> Satan seeks to draw our minds away from the mighty Helper, to lead us to ponder over our degeneration of soul. But though Jesus sees the guilt of the past, He speaks pardon; and we should not dishonor Him by doubting His love. *The feeling of guiltiness must be laid at the foot of the cross, or it will poison the springs of life.* When Satan thrusts his threatenings upon you, turn from them, and comfort your soul with the promises of God…. *God's children are not to be subject to feelings and emotions.* When they fluctuate between hope and fear, the heart of Christ is hurt; for He has given them unmistakable evidence of His love (*Messages to Young People*, pp. 109, 110, emphasis mine).

You may say, "But I *deserve* to feel guilty because I

have sinned after conversion." Who hasn't? Are you to lay your feelings of guilt at the foot of the cross only once? Are you thinking you are lost because you have sinned again? Are you implying there is no room for a saint to sin? Are you asking, "Am I saved by Christ, but now I am kept by my works? And if my works fail, am I lost?" Did David lose his salvation when he sinned a very great sin, which he did more than once. There were many smaller ones not recorded. Yes, there are degrees of sin. The Bible only recorded his major sins. So what do we do?

The prayers in the psalms are not just pleadings. They are promises that God will do what is asked. "Create in me a clean heart, O God, and renew a steadfast spirit within me. Do not cast me away from Your presence, and do not take Your Holy Spirit from me" (Ps. 51:10, 11).

God's mercy is not a once in a lifetime event. God realizes that His people will sin, or He wouldn't have inspired Ellen White to write the following:

> There are those who have known the pardoning love of Christ, and who really desire to be children of God, yet they realize that their character is imperfect, their life faulty, and they are ready to doubt whether their hearts have been renewed by the Holy spirit. To such I would say, Do not draw back in despair. *We shall often have to bow down and weep at the feet of Jesus because of our shortcomings and mistakes,* but we are not to be discouraged. Even if we are overcome by the enemy, we are not cast off, not forsaken and rejected of God (*Steps to Christ,* p. 64, emphasis mine).

Often have to bow down, often have to bow down! God actually knows we will give in to our weaknesses and make mistakes. Not that He wants us to, but He knows the reality of our messed up brains. So how do we handle the haunting deeds of the past and the failures of the present? Paul gave us a formula in Philippians 3:13, 14: "Brethren, I do not count myself to have apprehended; but one thing I do, *forgetting those things which are behind* and reaching forward to those things which are ahead, I press toward the goal."

Paul had a lot of forgetting to do. What Jesus did for Paul finally hit home for the young man who as a little boy learned to steal and lie and cheat. Surely if God could forgive Saul, He could forgive him, too.

Our problem is that we carry in our memories our past and our guilt, which can lead to a sense of hopeless despair, so that we subliminally resign ourselves to be lost. Our problem is outlined by Ellen White in *Testimonies for the Church*: "You do not trust enough in Jesus, precious Jesus. You do not make His worthiness to be all, all. The very best you can do will not merit the favor of God. It is Jesus' worthiness that will save you ... Confound not faith and feeling together. They are distinct. Faith is ours to exercise.... Your feelings have nothing to do with this faith. When faith brings the blessing to your heart, and you rejoice in the blessing, it is no more faith, but feeling" (vol. 1, p. 167).

Faith is grasping the perfect righteousness of Jesus put to your account, so that you need not feel the guilt any more. In fact, you are to lay your guilt at the foot of the cross.

It's almost too much to believe that no matter how bad we have been, no matter how many mistakes we still make, and no matter how unworthy we now feel, we are still saved by the matchless grace of God. Just as we put up with our children making mistake after mistake in learning to walk, so the Lord puts up with us learning to walk the Christlike walk. But that is what grace does. It loves. It forgives. It loves to forgive seventy times seven. Limitless when we confess! It restores, getting us ready for heaven.

There is a passage in *The Ministry of Healing* that should be helpful if you understand that God does not require of us something that He does not require of Himself. The passage is about an alcoholic who is really down and out. The attitudes God tells us to have toward this worthless hunk of human flesh (those are my words) are the same attitudes God has toward us in our own weaknesses. I will put in italics the words I want you to focus on.

> In dealing with the victims of intemperance we must remember that we are not dealing with sane men, but with those who for the time being are under the power of a demon. Be patient and forbearing. Think not of the repulsive, forbidding appearance, but of the precious life that Christ died to redeem. As the drunkard awakens to a sense of his degradation, do all in your power to show that you are his friend. *Speak no word of censure. Let no act or look express reproach or aversion.* Very likely the poor soul curses himself. Help him to rise. Speak words that will encourage faith. Seek to

strengthen every good trait in his character. Teach him how to reach upward (pp. 172, 173, emphasis mine).

When he curses himself, he probably thinks God is cursing him too. But God is speaking no words of censure and not acting or looking at him or you with reproach or aversion. He is looking sympathetically and encouragingly. The passage continues with truths that should help us to sense what God is doing for us.

> You must hold fast to those whom you are try-ing to help, else victory will never be yours. They will be continually tempted to evil. Again and again they will be almost overcome by the craving for strong drink; again and again *they may fall*; *but do not, because of this, cease your efforts* (Ibid., p. 173, emphasis mine).

And that is what our Lord Jesus is doing for us during the investigative judgment that is going on right now. It might have been better if it were not called the "investigative" judgment since He is doing more than investigating the records. He is judging the living, which means He is teaching us, delivering us, trying to persuade us to let Him rule over us, then eventually deciding our cases by ratifying our decisions. The four roles of a biblical judge will be made clear in the following chapters.

The quotations in this chapter are worth reading a second time. May you enjoy freedom as He delivers you from the things of the past, including the guilt of the past.

Even so, judge me please, and come, Lord Jesus!

Chapter 2

The Character of Christ

The purpose of writing this book is to expand our understanding of Christ's sanctuary ministry during the investigative judgment. In so doing, it will be helpful to explore what is meant by the character of Christ, because Christ's character has a lot to do with His role as judge.

Many of the quotations from Ellen White that I use in this chapter have been interpreted, or misinterpreted, in the past to indicate that sinless perfection is required in the last generation before Jesus comes. At no time is such a state of perfection required. We must read her statements carefully and consider them in light of these statements as I present them in this chapter.

Character

"When the character of Christ shall be perfectly reproduced in His people, then He will come to claim them as His own" (*Christ's Object Lessons,* p. 69). Apparently there is a condition that must be met before Christ can return—the character of Christ must be "perfectly reproduced in His people." Where is that idea in Scripture?

Then I looked, and behold, a white cloud, and on the cloud sat One like the Son of Man, having on His head a golden crown, and in His hand a sharp sickle. And another angel came out of the temple, crying with a loud voice to Him who sat on the cloud, "Thrust in Your sickle and reap, for the time has come for You to reap, *for the harvest of the earth is ripe*" (Rev. 14:14, 15).

Ripeness is the condition. There comes a time when the harvest of the earth is *ripe* for harvest. But *ripen* in what way? Earlier in the chapter we see a reference to something that can ripen—"firstfruits" (verse 4). The 144,000 are described as the "firstfruits" to God and to the Lamb. The 144,000 are ripened by the three angels' messages shortly before Jesus returns. In what way do they ripen?

They ripen in character. The very next verse reads, "And in their mouth was found no deceit, for they are without fault before the throne of God" (verse 5). Thoughts, feelings, behavior are the components of character. No deceit in their mouth is behavior that comes from their faultless character. A character without fault is the same as the character of Christ. While it is true that imparted righteousness is developed by continually accepting Christ's imputed righteousness, so that one can say a faultless character comes from both imputed and imparted righteousness, in this case, "without fault" is more imparted righteousness since it is an absence of deceit in their hearts, minds, and mouths. It is the character of Christ reproduced in them. The exact meaning of the "character of Christ" will be defined a little later.

Notice in passing that the character of the wicked has also ripened (verse 18). The events that take place under the rule of the beast and its image harden hearts and fix the character of its followers. Those testing events bring about a sifting that shakes the tares out from the wheat, leaving a strikingly visible contrast. No one can stay in the remnant church at that time unless they are sealed, truly settled into the faith. And those who leave will harden their hearts and become bitter enemies of the truth.

The perfect reproduction of Christ in the church can also be found in Ephesians 4, where the gifts of the Spirit are given for that very purpose, "till we all come to the unity of the faith and of the knowledge of the Son of God, to a perfect man, to the measure of the stature of the fullness of Christ" (verse 13).

Remember, when talking about the 144,000, we are not talking about individual salvation. That is a gift. We are talking about a demonstration accomplished during the investigative judgment that gives God the right (justification) to destroy Satan and his followers, completing the atonement and the plan of salvation.

The Character of Christ

"When the character of Christ shall be perfectly reproduced in His people, then He will come to claim them as His own" (*Christ's Object Lessons,* p. 69).

So what is the character of Christ? Is it sinlessness? Is it His perfect obedience to the law? Must we obey perfectly before Jesus can "come to claim them as His own"? Let's explore this topic.

Since I will use terms like sinless, righteous, and perfect, it seems fitting that we examine these terms from a biblical viewpoint.

Righteousness

According to the Bible, there *are* righteous people.

1. John the Baptist's parents, Zacharias and Elizabeth, "were both righteous before God, walking in all the commandments and ordinances of the Lord blameless" (Luke 1:6).

2. Twice God says of Job, "there is none like him on the earth, a blameless and upright man, one who fears God and shuns evil" (Job 1:8; 2:3). If he was blameless, then he was righteous. And that was the testimony about him in spite of all that Satan did to him: "In all this Job did not sin nor charge God with wrong" (Job 1:22). It might be prudent to note the words, "in all this." In so far as this test was concerned, Job did not sin. I wouldn't want to stretch the statement to suggest that Job never sinned before or after this.

3. In Ezekiel there are three who were named righteous: "'Even if these three men, Noah, Daniel, and Job, were in it, they would deliver only themselves by their righteousness,' says the Lord GOD" (Ezek. 14:14).

4. Also, consider Abel (Matt. 23:35) and Noah (Gen. 6:9-7:1).

So, according to the Bible, there have been and will

be righteous people. But what did Paul mean then when he wrote, "There is none righteous, no, not one" (Rom. 3:10)? It might appear that he meant everyone, thereby contradicting the references above. But in the appendix, you will learn that the Bible's usage of *all, none, every* are seldom used in their absolute sense.

But more importantly, Paul is quoting from Psalm 14:1-3 where David is describing the "children of men" who deny the existence of God and are wicked because of it:

> The fool has said in his heart, "There is no God." They are corrupt, they have done abominable works, there is none who does good. The LORD looks down from heaven upon the children of men, to see if there are any who understand, who seek God. They have all turned aside, they have together become corrupt; There is none who does good, No, not one.

The "children of men" (verse 2) usually refers to the wicked in contrast to the "children of God," the righteous. Paul knows as he writes to the Romans that there are righteous people, for he writes in Romans 8:4 "that the righteous requirement of the law might be fulfilled in us who do not walk according to the flesh but according to the Spirit," so Paul is not contradicting Luke's testimony about Zacharias and Elizabeth.

The contrast between the children of men and the children of God is significant because before the flood the sons of God saw the daughters of men and they took beautiful, but corrupt, wives for themselves which led to the destruction of the earth by the flood.

In Psalm 14:2, 3 David wrote, "The LORD looks down from heaven upon *the children of men*, to see if there is any who understand, *who seeks God*" (emphasis mine). David then gives the results of God's search, "They have all turned aside, they have together become corrupt; there is none who does good, no, not one." When David wrote "they have all turned aside," he was reporting God's search and saying, in essence, there are none "who seeks after God." That is because both David and Paul are writing about the children of men. The children of God are not the corrupt ones. They do seek God. So, without contradicting Psalm 14, David wrote in other places:

- Let all those who seek You rejoice and be glad in You (Ps. 40:16).
- Blessed are those who keep His testimonies, who seek Him with the whole heart! (Ps. 119:2).
- As the deer pants for the water brooks, so pants my soul for You, O God. My soul thirsts for God, for the living God (Ps. 42:1, 2).

And Jude wrote, "Now to Him who is able to keep you from stumbling, and to present you faultless before the presence of His glory with exceeding joy" (verse 24). "Faultless" is pretty righteous. Jude's "faultless" nature is imparted righteousness because it follows immediately after, "to keep you from stumbling," which is behavior. So there are righteous people, but are they sinless?

"Houston, we have a problem"—Sinlessness

Some people may not like what I write here, but

I challenge them to show me one person who fits the demands of absolute sinlessness. It has been my experience that even when I am around one of God's finest saints it doesn't take long to discern traits that fall short of at least my expectation of a perfect character.

In addition to what I *think* has been my experience, the overarching backdrop of my bias in writing this section is found in 1 John and statements from Ellen White. There will never come a time this side of heaven when these statements aren't true. Let's examine them.

"If we say that we have no sin, we deceive ourselves, and the truth is not in us" (1 John 1:8). If we have sin, then we are not sinless. Consider this quote from Ellen White:

> We should carefully consider what is our relation to God and to one another. We are continually sinning against God, but his mercy still follows us; in love he bears with our perversities, our neglect, our ingratitude, our disobedience (*The Review and Herald,* October 31, 1912).

If we are continually sinning, then we aren't sinless. That goes for Zacharias, Elizabeth, Job, Noah, and Daniel. So, that leads me to conclude that we can be righteous without being sinless.

Even if I were not guilty of sins of commission, which is not true, I am certainly guilty of sins of omission. So many things left undone and unsaid!

> We should remember that our own ways are not faultless. We make mistakes again and again.... No one is perfect but Jesus. Think of

Him and be charmed away from yourself, and from every disagreeable thing, for by beholding our defects faith is weakened (*That I May Know Him*, p. 136).

[Christ] is a perfect and holy example, given for us to imitate. We cannot equal the pattern; but we shall not be approved of God if we do not copy it and, according to the ability which God has given, resemble it (*Testimonies for the Church*, vol. 2, p. 549).

Notice what Ellen White says about "true believers" in *Selected Messages*. "The religious services, the prayers, the praise, the penitent confession of sin ascend from true believers as incense to the heavenly sanctuary, but passing through *the corrupt channels of humanity*, they are so defiled that unless purified by blood, they can never be of value with God. They ascend not in spotless purity, and unless the Intercessor, who is at God's right hand, presents and purifies all by His righteousness, it is not acceptable to God (book 1, p. 344, emphasis mine). "Since we are sinful, unholy, we cannot perfectly obey the holy law" (*Steps to Christ*, p. 62).

It could be argued that she is describing man before conversion, but because of the overall intent of the passage, I would apply this statement to both before and after conversion.

This sinful, unholy nature stays with us right alongside our new nature received at conversion, and it wars against the new nature, keeping us from sinless obedience.

So then, what is this character of Christ that must be

perfectly reproduced in His people and for which heaven is waiting with longing desire to see in His church? The following quotation, which applies more to *our* characters than to Christ's, begins to answer the question. "The character [ours] is revealed, not by occasional good deeds and occasional misdeeds, but by the tendency of the habitual words and acts" (*Steps to Christ*, pp. 57, 58).

Tendency conveys direction and slant. Character in the visual sense is represented best by an arrow pointing upward, implying direction and movement. Character does not have an endpoint but will continue to grow infinitely in heaven.

> A character formed according to the divine likeness is the only treasure that we can take from this world to the next. Those who are under the instruction of Christ in this world will take every divine attainment with them to the heavenly mansions. And in heaven we are continually to improve. How important, then, is the development of character in this life (*Christ's Object Lessons,* p. 332).

Note that before Christ returns the character of God's people is fixed (Rev. 22:11). "Fixed" means their characters will not change *direction* after this. "Fixed" does not mean that their characters will not grow, but that the direction of their characters will not change. The righteous will remain righteous, and the wicked will remain wicked. Likely the characters of the wicked will grow also. They will grow worse and worse for just a little while before and after the millennium.

From the *Steps to Christ* statement above, I would infer that a character trending upward can commit misdeeds that do not make him unrighteous, which is consistent with the statement, "We shall often have to bow down and weep at the feet of Jesus because of our shortcomings and mistakes" (*Steps to Christ*, p. 64). That statement is made to converted people. God fully expects His converted people to make mistakes, sinful mistakes, and often. That should be a relief to those who think they must be absolutely sinless in order to go to heaven.

God's statement to Solomon about his father is helpful here: "Now if you walk before Me as your father David walked, in integrity of heart and in uprightness..." (1 Kings 9:4). The life of David was anything but sinless, yet he is described as one who has integrity of heart and uprightness. How? The *big* difference between David with all his mistakes and Solomon with all his mistakes is that David's heart never turned from the Lord, while Solomon's wives turned his heart to serve other gods.

In chapter 5 you will see that David wanted to be judged. It was not because he was sinless, but because he trusted in God honestly with singleness of heart in spite of his faulty ways. "Judge me, O LORD, according to my righteousness, and according to my integrity within me" (Ps. 7:8). "Vindicate [judge] me, O LORD, for I have walked in my integrity. I have also trusted in the LORD; I shall not slip" (Ps. 26:1).

Serving the Lord and only the Lord is the critical choice the faultless, righteous 144,000 make more than never committing sin. The last generation is settled into the faith with undeviating loyalty so that they shall not slip away from the truth, so that they cannot be moved out of their allegiance to God no matter what.

Biblical Perfection

Biblical perfection is not sinlessness. "Though He was a Son, yet He learned obedience by the things which He suffered. And having been perfected, He became the author of eternal salvation to all who obey Him" (Heb. 5:8, 9).

Jesus was sinless from birth, yet He had to be perfected. If perfection means sinlessness, how can a sinless being be made sinless in the process of being made perfect? Read Hebrews 2:10: "For it was fitting for Him, for whom are all things and by whom are all things, in bringing many sons to glory, to make the captain of their salvation perfect through sufferings."

This sinless Being had to be made perfect. In what way was He made perfect? When Jesus was a child, He thought as a child, behaved as a child, yet without sin. But He still needed to grow physically, mentally, and spiritually (Luke 2:52). He matured in thinking, in wisdom, and especially in His dedication and commitment to His Father and to His Father's mission for Him. When He was twelve, at the Passover, Jesus recognized Himself in the sacrifices, and He surrendered His future to His Father. But that dedication had to be tested, proven, and galvanized through various temptations and tests. *His perfection for all the universes to see was His undeviating and absolute commitment to God and to His mission so that he could not be dissuaded.* Through the many life experiences He endured, His character, His direction in life, was proven. He demonstrated that He was singularly loyal to His Father, and could not be led to worship the devil, nor be turned aside from His Father's declared mission for Him, even by crucifixion if there was no other way to save the human race—"Not My will, but Yours, be done."

No question! Christ was sinless. He did not sin (1 Pet. 2:22). But His sinlessness was not His character. It was the result of His character, which was revealed in His habitual words and acts. It was the result of His conscious choice to please His Father. The question for us is, "Who has the heart?" (*Steps to Christ*, p. 58). God the Father had Christ's heart. It was Christ's delight to please His Father, to live for Him, to continue to choose Him, and to surrender His will to His Father's prescribed plan for Him that enabled Him to live an undeviating life along with His connection to His Father that He had from birth. *This undeviating commitment is biblical perfection.*

God's people are to have that same undeviating love and choice and direction in their lives. I cannot improve on this precious statement already penned for us:

> The loveliness of the character of Christ will be seen in His followers. It was His delight to do the will of God. Love to God, zeal for His glory, was the controlling power in our Saviour's life. Love beautified and ennobled all His actions. Love is of God. The uncon-secrated heart cannot originate or produce it. It is found only in the heart where Jesus reigns. "We love, because He first loved us." 1 John 4:19, R.V. In the heart renewed by di-

vine grace, love is the principle of action. It modifies the character, governs the impulses, controls the passions, subdues enmity, and ennobles the affections. This love, cherished in the soul, sweetens the life and sheds a refining influence on all around (*Steps to Christ,* p. 59).

This love and unction by the Holy Spirit will lead quite naturally to obedience to God's law, albeit, not perfectly as we usually use the term. We will exert our wills to resist sin and overcome our old natures that clamor for attention. This exertion is a response to the Holy Spirit who is creating this desire to overcome, and is pushing/pulling us in an upward direction. If we desire with all our heart to serve God and act on that desire so that our words and actions show a righteous tendency, I propose that we *have the character of Christ.* We have biblical perfection. So what is the character of Christ perfectly reproduced in His people?

It is when His people are fixed on the upward way. It is when they would rather die than sin. It is when they are so settled into the faith that they cannot be moved—they are sealed. The contortions of the last days will do their work of weeding out those who do not have this character. But there are those who will not be shaken from the Adventist faith, not even by the threat of death or starvation or worse, the starvation of their children, which will come upon them by the beast and its image. Mind you, this is only a threat, for our bread and water will be sure.

The shaking experience that the remnant will go through will strip away the vestiges of any sins that may have been bothering them and will develop a church full of people who are perfect (perfectly committed), yet they will be the last to claim it, because the closer they come to Christ the more unworthy they will appear in their own eyes. Thus, we cannot tell when we are fit for heaven. We are not to judge ourselves or others. God and God alone will do that. But we can hang our helpless, unworthy souls on Him who died for us that we might live. When we do this, He, as the Author and Finisher of our faith, will "keep [us] from stumbling, and present [us] faultless before the presence of His glory with exceeding joy" (Jude 24).

Additional Support

Now I want to present another way of looking at some Bible texts that are usually used to insist on perfect sinlessness.

If you are tempted to think that everyone who goes to heaven must be perfectly sinless, remember the thief on the cross. Always remember the thief on the cross—the greatest illustration of salvation by grace and grace alone. I'm sure he had a lot of flaws, but he had no more time to eliminate them. He will do that in Paradise where there is no tempter.

Yes, I know, the 144,000 have more time and more light in the pure Adventist doctrines to grow beyond the thief on the cross, but even then, they cannot rise above the statements and texts made earlier in this chapter that we are all sinners who are continually sinning.

In Hebrews 10:26, 27 we read, "For if we sin willfully after we have received the knowledge of the truth, there no longer remains a sacrifice for sins, but a fearful expectation of judgment, and fiery indignation which will devour the adversaries." Except for some sin of ignorance, I think I have always known when I was sinning, and I obviously did it willfully, consentingly, even after I was converted. Does that mean there is no more sacrifice for me? No. John says to the converted, "If anyone sins, we have an Advocate with the Father," so there is hope.

Furthermore, "We shall often have to bow down and weep at the feet of Jesus because of our shortcomings and mistakes [sins], but ... *we are not cast off*" (*Steps to Christ*, p. 64, emphasis mine). How then are we to understand these texts in Hebrews? When Paul writes "if we sin willfully," He is *not* talking about the occasional misdeed, or even being *overcome* by the enemy. He is talking about the unpardonable sin when one willfully, deliberately, and knowingly turns his back on God and truth for the last time, because the same verse says that for this person there no longer remains a sacrifice for sin (Heb. 10:26). He is totally exposed. No hope for him. He will die in his sins, in his rejection of God and the truth.

But, notice that the opposite of willfully committing sin is staying in the faith. In the preceding verses Paul writes, "Let us hold fast the confession of our hope without wavering, for He who promised is faithful" (verse 23). Then follows instruction, "And let us consider one another in order to stir up love and good works, not forsaking the assembling of ourselves together, as is the manner of some, but exhorting one another, and so much the more as you see the Day approaching, For if we sin willfully..." (verses

33

24-26). We are to meet more often than once a week, "so much the more as you see the Day approaching," for the purpose of encouraging one another so that we do not sin willfully, i.e. fall away from Christ. Staying in the faith is the goal and the exhortation. He ends the chapter with this thought, "We are not of those who draw back to perdition, but of those who believe to the saving of the soul" (verse 39).

It is the same in an earlier passage where Paul is talking about people who have completely rejected the offer of grace. "For it is impossible for those who were once enlightened, and have tasted the heavenly gift, and have become partakers of the Holy Spirit, and have tasted the good word of God and the powers of the age to come, if they fall away, to renew them again to repentance, since they crucify again for themselves the Son of God, and put Him to an open shame" (Heb. 6:4-6).

In this passage, to "fall away" is to fall away from the faith completely because the passage has within it its own limitation—"It is impossible." Therefore the passage is talking about people who have grieved away the Holy Spirit completely, not people who are struggling to obey Christ and their conscience, yet making mistakes.

Staying in the faith is also the emphasis at the beginning of Hebrews. Chapter 2, verses 1-3 uses such words as "drift" and "neglect," and chapter 3, verse 6 uses the phrase "hold fast."

Let's look more closely at Jude where honor is ascribed to "Him who is able to keep you from stumbling, and to present you faultless" (verse 24). Suppose we interpret this text this way, "Now to Him who is able to keep you from stumbling [*out of the faith*], and [therefore] to present you faultless [by His imputed righteousness, which He does for all believers] before the presence of His glory with exceeding joy." I suggest this reading because in verse 21 Jude writes, "keep yourselves in the love of God [in the faith], looking for the *mercy* [not perfection] of our Lord Jesus Christ unto eternal life." The emphasis is more on remaining in the faith than on sinlessness. If we stay in the faith, in the church where the gifts are, and do our best in spite of all our inherited and cultivated weaknesses, God will see us through. If we separate ourselves from the church and pull away from all the exhortations and spiritual gifts, we *will* backslide and may eventually be lost.

I think the same emphasis is seen in Paul's final letter to Timothy where he writes, "I have fought the good fight, I have finished the race, I have kept the faith" (2 Tim. 4:7). "I have kept the faith." He doesn't suggest that he is ready for translation or that he is perfect. In fact he writes to the Philippians, "Not that I have already attained, or am already perfected; but I press on" (Phil. 3:12).

In his letter to Timothy, Paul is very concerned about doctrine. He warns against those who have strayed concerning the truth that their message will spread like cancer (2 Tim. 2:15-18). A little later he wrote that "the time will come when they will not endure sound doctrine" (2 Tim. 4:3). Paul knew that what we believe about God affects our relationship to God.

The thought of pure doctrine and becoming like Christ is found in Ephesians 4, where the spiritual gifts are given to bring us to "a perfect man, to the measure of the stature of the fullness of Christ: *that we should no longer be children, tossed to and fro and carried about with every wind of doctrine, by the trickery of men, in the cunning craftiness of deceitful plotting, but, speaking the truth in love, may grow up in all things into Him who is the head–Christ*" (verse 13-15, emphasis mine).

Pure doctrine brings me to a final thought along this line. In Revelation 14 the 144,000 are described as having no deceit in their mouths, for they are without fault. In the context, "no deceit in their mouths" can apply to the pure doctrines His people proclaim as compared to the false, deceptive doctrines proclaimed by the beast and its image. The margin reads "no falsehood" in their mouths. Pure doctrine produces pure people.

Some people react to the word "doctrine." But "God is love" is doctrine. John 3:16 is doctrine. Pure doctrine includes God's plan of salvation and the destruction of the wicked. So, pure doctrine produces pure people. It includes conversion. It includes "we love Him because He first loved us." So out of love and gratitude to God for all He has done for their restoration His people stay in the faith, purify themselves, and glorify their Creator and Redeemer.

Pure doctrine is another reason God has given the gift of prophecy to the remnant church. The many false doctrines permeating Christianity have so badly misrepresented God that thinking people are turned away from Him rather than being drawn to Him. The Spirit of Prophecy assured our pioneers that they were on the right track in holding to truths different from the falsehoods of popular Christianity, in adopting the historic view of prophecy, and in discovering the sanctuary truth with its high calling to His remnant people.

It's time we become so committed to God that we welcome and embrace all the practical godliness truths that in mercy He has given us from the Most Holy Place, truths by which He is purifying His people. I want to be one of those people. How about you?

Chapter 3

Good News of the Judgment

My journey into the investigative judgment began with two intriguing quotations:

> Had Adventists, after the great disappointment in 1844, held fast their faith, and followed on unitedly in the opening providence of God, receiving the message of the third angel and in the power of the Holy Spirit proclaiming it to the world, they would have seen the salvation of God, the Lord would have wrought mightily with their efforts, the work would have been completed, and *Christ would have come ere this to receive His people to their reward* (*Selected Messages,* book 1, p. 68, emphasis mine).

The "Adventists" mentioned above refers to the whole of the Millerite believers, not to the small remnant of Seventh-day Adventists organized twenty years later. Nevertheless, the statement remains that Christ could have come before 1883. Then I compared the above quotation with the following:

> The judgment is now passing in the sanctuary above. For many years this work has been in progress. Soon—none know how soon—it will

pass to the cases of the living. In the awful [awe-
some] presence of God our lives are to come up
in review (*The Great Controversy,* p. 490).

The judgment Ellen White is referring to is what we
call the investigative judgment that began in 1844 and
must be completed before Jesus returns. Therefore, it
seems to me that if Christ could have come before 1883
judgment should have passed to the living long ago. So,
what does it mean to pass from the cases of the dead to the
cases of the living? Will something happen on earth when
it does? What difference does it make to those living on
earth when it does?

Other questions come to mind. What difference does
1844 make to one born in 1740 or in 1940? What difference
does it make to our individual salvation whether Christ is
in the holy place or the Most Holy Place? These questions
are asked not just to raise questions. Sometimes asking
the right questions helps us discover the right answers,
especially when seeking more light.

Consider this statement in *Selected Messages*, "It is
the unbelief, the worldliness, unconsecration, and strife
among the Lord's professed people that have kept us in
this world of sin and sorrow so many years" (book 1, p. 69).

That statement implies that *we* are the ones delaying
Christ's coming. Might it also imply that *we* are delaying
the completion of the judgment? But that is not the focus
of this chapter.

Back to the good news of the judgment. When you read
such statements as, "In the awful presence of God our lives
are to come up in review," and you read in 2 Corinthians

10:5 that "we must all appear before the judgment seat of Christ," do you look forward to your name coming up in the judgment? Do you view the judgment with enthusiasm and excitement or with dread and foreboding?

Revelation 14:6 reads, "I saw another angel flying in the midst of heaven, having the everlasting gospel to preach to those who dwell on the earth—to every nation, tribe, tongue, and people." Most evangelists stop there and ask the audience, "What is the everlasting gospel?" The response usually is "Jesus died for our sins, etc." But that is the gospel of Jesus Christ, not the everlasting gospel. The everlasting gospel cannot be completed without the gospel of Jesus. But the everlasting gospel embraces more than the central gospel of Jesus the Messiah.

The everlasting gospel takes us all the way to the lost dominion restored. When God placed Adam in the garden, He gave him dominion over the earth. But when Adam failed to trust God, he forfeited that dominion into the hands of Satan. The image of God in man was sullied. The everlasting gospel is not completed until the image of God is restored in man and dominion is returned to the human race and sin and sinners are no more. When the everlasting gospel is completed peace and harmony will once again reign throughout God's vast creation. I am not diminishing the gospel of Jesus Christ. The incarnation, life, and death of Jesus and His resurrection, ascension, and intercession in the courts above are vital to accomplishing the everlasting gospel, but it is only part of the gospel. The judgment is the rest.

The term "gospel" means "good news." The gospel of

Jesus is the good news about Jesus. The everlasting gospel is also by definition *good news*. So when the first angel of Revelation 14 brings the everlasting gospel, he is bringing good news. At the risk of repeating myself, notice that when John "saw another angel ... having the *everlasting gospel* to preach to those who dwell on the earth," the angel was not telling the story of Jesus (verse 6). When he opens his mouth, he says "with a loud voice, 'Fear God and give glory to Him, for the hour of His judgment has come'" (verse 7).

So, the message of the judgment is by definition good news, really good news. It is something for which to give glory to God. It is something for which to fear or revere God. We are to stand in awe of Him, marvel at Him, admire Him, love Him, worship Him, and be filled with wonder at His character. We are to honor Him because He has begun the judgment. And we are to proclaim this to the world as good news, wonderful news.

We should note that this announcement of the judgment is not talking about the end of the world and God's judgment on the wicked, because after proclaiming that "the hour of His judgment has come," there follows a command to worship the Creator, so there is time to respond to this message before the end of the world.

But what makes the announcement of the judgment good news? Let's look at Daniel 7 where the answer is given three times, which may raise even more intriguing questions. Three times in Daniel 7, the kingdom/dominion is taken from the ruling powers and given to the saints of the Most High, twice as a result of the judgment.

41

Those great beasts, which are four, are four
kings which arise out of the earth. But the
saints of the Most High shall receive the kingdom, and possess the kingdom forever, even
forever and ever.... I was watching; and the
same horn was making war against the saints,
and prevailing against them, until the Ancient
of Days came, and a judgment was made *in
favor* of the saints of the Most High, and the
time came for the saints to possess the kingdom.... But the court shall be seated, and they
shall take away his [the little horn's] dominion,
to consume and destroy it forever. Then the
kingdom and dominion, and the greatness of
the kingdoms under the whole heaven, shall
be given to the people, the saints of the Most
High. His kingdom is an everlasting kingdom,
and all dominions shall serve and obey Him
(verses 17-27).

This judgment in Daniel 7 is the same investigative
judgment or pre-advent judgment proclaimed in
Revelation 14. Because the Ancient of Days, the Father,
is seated on His moveable throne, the court or judgment
is called into session and the books are opened (Dan. 7:9,
10). Next, "One like the Son of Man, coming with the
clouds of heaven," comes not to this earth as at the second
coming, but is brought before the Ancient of Days (verse
13). This judgment takes place in heaven *before* Jesus
returns. And as a result of this judgment, the kingdom/
dominion is taken from the little horn and given to the
saints of the Most High. So, by all means give glory to Him
for the hour of His judgment has come.

Importance of the Judgment-Hour Message

The judgment hour message and the year 1844 must be extremely important because God uses three major lines of prophecy leading up to the investigative judgment and then proclaims the judgment as part of the last warning message to the world.

As mentioned earlier, when the first angel of Revelation 14:6, 7 opens his mouth to proclaim the everlasting gospel, he says among other things, "the hour of His judgment has come." This message is obviously of great importance because it is one of the three final warning messages to the world. And it includes a call to worship the Creator instead of accepting the godless theory of evolution. This issue is itself a major controversy in the last days, raising the judgment hour message even higher.

Consider the following thoughts about the judgment-hour message as announced by the first angel.

2300 Days Opens the Judgment

The Millerite movement based on the 2300 days of Daniel 8:14 caused a large-scale awakening in America and around the world, which led to the remnant receiving a revelation that Christ had entered into the Most Holy Place in 1844 to begin the investigative judgment.

Cosmic Signs Announce the Judgment

We have used the cosmic signs as signs of Christ's second coming. That's okay for Matthew 24, but the cosmic signs under the sixth seal really announce the investigative judgment (Rev. 6:12). They are a response to the saints' appeal under the fifth seal, "How long, O Lord, holy and true, until You judge...?" (verse 10). The 144,000 of Revelation 7 not only stand in the judgment but are the very ones to proclaim the judgment-hour message of Revelation 14:6, 7.

A similar sequence is seen in Joel. Remember that in the first angel's message of Revelation 14:6, 7, after announcing that the judgment has come, a call is made to worship the Creator. Therefore, after announcing that the judgment has come, there is time for people to turn to the Lord. Likewise in Joel, after the cosmic signs, there is time for deliverance of a remnant who call upon the name of the Lord.

> And I will show wonders in the heavens and in the earth: Blood and fire and pillars of smoke [wars]. The sun shall be turned into darkness, and the moon into blood, before the coming of the great and awesome day of the LORD. And it shall come to pass that whoever calls on the name of the LORD shall be saved. For in Mount Zion and in Jerusalem there shall be deliverance, As the LORD has said, among the remnant whom the LORD calls (Joel 2:30-32).

Investigative Judgment Defeats the Little Horn

Chapter 7 of Daniel contains one of the greatest prophecies in the Bible, predicting the rise and fall of nations and introducing the little horn who was to rule the world for 1260 years, and rule again as the beast of Revelation 13 after it recovers from its lethal wound. The little horn of Daniel 7, which is "the man of sin" of 2 Thessalonians 3:2 and the first beast of Revelation 13, is a major, major player in the great controversy between Christ and Satan.

The investigative judgment takes away the little horn's rule in its second phase as the first beast of Revelation 13, which makes the investigative judgment a very important event in the great controversy between Christ and Satan, thus making 1844 a very important date in that controversy.

Convergences

After 6,000 years of Bible history, the convergences of these major lines of Bible prophecy coming together just before 1844, as seen in the diagram below, scream out that something momentous happened in God's plan of salvation that year. Assuming you are familiar with the events in the diagram (See Figure 1), I will not recite them here. I will only name each with their dates.

2300 days ─────────

───── 1260 days ─────

1755	1780	1798	1833	1844
Lisbon Earthquake	Dark Day	Papal Wound	Star Shower	Investigative Judgment Begins

Figure 1

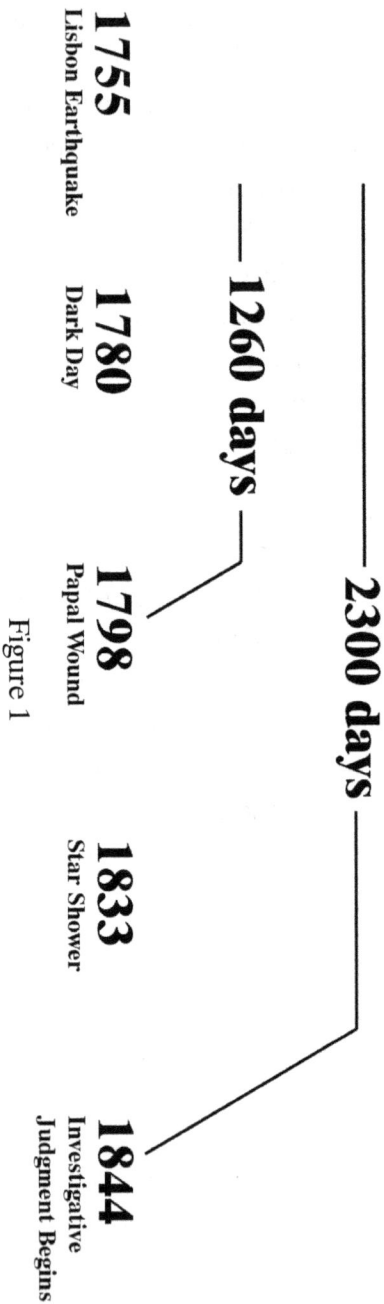

Those converging lines of prophecy are even more arresting when we add the rise of the second beast of Revelation 13:

- 1776 – signing of the Declaration of Independence
- 1787 – framing of the U.S. Constitution
- 1789 – election of the first U.S. president

God brought together several lines of prophecy to make sure His people did not miss 1844. Plus He gave the gift of prophecy to guide His remnant church beginning in 1844.

The Paramount Question

For years, when giving a Bible study on Daniel 7, I would build a parallel between the different metals of Daniel 2 and the four great beasts—Babylon, Medo-Persia, Greece, and Rome. I felt that this was reasonable, but when the scenes of the judgment got in the way of my parallel, I would tell my students, "A judgment is portrayed here, but I will cover that at another time," and I would proceed with the parallel. My students always seemed to accept my statement at face value. They never asked *why* about the judgment. Then one day I asked myself why. I decided it was time to figure out *why* the scenes of the judgment kept interfering with my Bible study. The reason was obvious.

It is as a result of this judgment that the kingdom is taken from the little horn and given to the saints of the Most High: "The court shall be seated, and they shall take away his dominion" (verse 26). But the obvious and paramount question is, "What happens in the investigative judgment to justify taking the kingdom away from the little horn?"

Most have pictured the investigative judgment as Christ moving from the holy place to the Most Holy Place, and there going over the books of record to see who will go to heaven and who will not. And that's all. True, He *is* going over the books, but that is not all He is doing.

In Daniel 7, as a result of the judgment, Christ receives the kingdom from His Father, at which time He shares it with His saints. So again, what happens in this pre-advent judgment that gives God the right to take the

47

kingdom from the little horn and give it to His saints? It is not because of what Christ did 2,000 years ago or else the judgment and the transfer of power could have been completed then. Something more must be done. Consider another statement.

> The intercession of Christ in man's behalf in the sanctuary above is *as essential to the plan of salvation* as His death on the cross. By His death He *began* that work which after His resurrection He ascended to complete in heaven (*The Great Controversy*, p. 489, emphasis mine).

The words "essential" and "began" should be emphasized. Something more beyond Christ's earthly life and death must be accomplished to justify taking the kingdom from the powers of earth and giving it to the redeemed. And this *something* takes place during the second phase of Christ's sanctuary ministry, during the investigative judgment, which is glorious and marvelous.

So let me end this chapter asking the same question, "What happens in the investigative judgment to justify taking the kingdom away from the little horn?"

Chapter 4

A Biblical Judge

From Revelation 14:6, 7 we saw that the judgment-hour message is good news, and one reason is that as a result of the judgment (the investigative judgment) in Daniel 7 the saints receive the kingdom.

Now, for more "good news." In the courts of law in the United States, a judge sits behind a bench and makes decisions about guilt or innocence, pronouncing a sentence upon the guilty according to prescribed statutes. But a biblical judge does much more than a U.S. judge, and Jesus is a biblical judge.

Let's first establish that Jesus is a judge. Peter declares, God "commanded us to preach to the people, and to testify that it is He [Jesus] who was ordained by God to be Judge of the living and the dead" (Acts 10:42; see also Acts 17:31).

Jesus said, "The Father judges no one, but has committed all judgment to the Son" (John 5:22). His work as judge determines who goes to heaven and who doesn't, because in the previous verse, He said, "As the Father raises the dead and gives life to them, even so the Son gives life to whom He will" (verse 21). He continues:

For as the Father has life in Himself, so he has granted the Son to have life in Himself, and has given Him authority to execute judgment also, because He is the Son of Man. Do not marvel at this; for the hour is coming in which all who are in the graves will hear His voice and come forth—those who have done good, to the resurrection of life, and those who have done evil, to the resurrection of condemnation. I can of Myself do nothing. As I hear, I judge; and My judgment is righteous, because I do not seek My own will but the will of the Father who sent Me (verses 26-30).

Jesus is referring to the pre-advent judgment or what we refer to as the investigative judgment, because when Jesus returns, He already knows who will be resurrected and who will not.

There are two judgments following Christ's return. The first is what we would call in our legal system an appeal. Upon His return, it is as if the wicked, or even the righteous, appeal Christ's judgment. The righteous then have a thousand years to review the records to satisfy themselves that His judgment is just. The second is the executive judgment when the wicked are executed at the end of the millennium.

At one point Jesus said, "I judge no one," but He followed that with, "and yet if I do judge, My judgment is true; for I am not alone, but I am with the Father who sent Me" (John 8:15, 16). In this passage Jesus is talking about His life while on earth, not about the future when, in fact, He is our judge.

50

At another time Jesus said, "If anyone hears My words and does not believe, I do not judge him; for I did not come to judge the world but to save the world. He who rejects Me, and does not receive My words, has that which judges him—the word that I have spoken will judge him in the last day" (John 12:47, 48). Jesus is here stating an important truth that the *Word* is the standard by which we are judged. For Seventh-day Adventists today, the *Word* includes Christ Himself and *all* of Christ's teachings—the whole Bible and the writings of the Spirit of Prophecy, a spiritual gift given just to us.

The Four Functions of a Biblical Judge

The four functions of a biblical judge are to make decisions, teach, rule, and deliver. Reading from Exodus 18:16, Moses is explaining to his father-in-law, Jethro, what he does as judge: "When they have a difficulty, they come to me, and I judge between one and another."

And from Deuteronomy 1:16 Moses recites what he did when he appointed judges over the people according to Jethro's suggestion: "Then I commanded your judges at that time, saying, 'Hear the cases between your brethren, and judge righteously between a man and his brother or the stranger who is with him.'" Here the biblical judge does what we usually think a judge does. A biblical judge *decides*.

After telling Jethro that he (Moses) judges (decides), he then tells him, "And I make known the statutes of God and His laws" (Exod. 18:16b). Jethro then affirms that function as he tells Moses, "You shall teach them the statutes and the laws, and show them the way in which they must walk and the work they must do" (verse 20).

Moses was clearly teaching the children of Israel in Deuteronomy 4:1 when he said, "Now, O Israel, listen to the statutes and the judgments which I teach you to observe, that you may live, and go in and possess the land which the LORD God of your fathers is giving you."

Both as a prophet and as a judge, Moses was a great teacher. He received the commandments, statutes, and judgments as a prophet. He then taught those who might not have heard them in his role as judge. A biblical judge *teaches*.

Jethro continues his suggestions to Moses in Exodus 18:

> Moreover you shall select from all the people able men, such as fear God, men of truth, hating covetousness; and place such over them to be rulers of thousands, rulers of hundreds, rulers of fifties, and rulers of tens. And let them judge the peoples at all times. Then it will be that every great matter they shall bring to you, but every small matter they themselves shall judge.... And Moses chose able men out of all Israel, and made them heads over the people: rulers of thousands, rulers of hundreds, rulers of fifties, and rulers of tens (verses 21-25).

The book of Judges is replete with God calling someone to serve as judge who also ruled the children of Israel. But there came a time when the men of Israel grew tired of judges ruling them. They wanted a king to rule over them. By definition, a king rules!

But the king also judged. The people of Israel said to Samuel, "Look, you are old, and your sons do not walk in your ways. Now make us a king to judge us like all the nations" (1 Sam. 8:5). "Judge" and "rule" are virtually synonymous. "Now make us a king to judge us" is the same as "Make us a king to rule over us." Kings rule over their subjects.

Of God it is written, "Oh, let the nations be glad and sing for joy! For You shall *judge* the people righteously, and *govern* the nations on earth" (Ps. 67:4). A biblical judge *rules*.

But one of the more significant functions of a biblical judge is to deliver. The book of Judges is called Judges for a reason. Over and over in the book of Judges, God raised up a judge to *deliver* the children of Israel from their enemies.

The children of Israel repeatedly turned from God to worship idols, so God sometimes allowed and sometimes brought disaster and or captivity upon them. "Nevertheless, the LORD raised up judges who *delivered* them out of the hand of those who plundered them" (Judg. 2:16).

As an example, "The children of Israel did evil in the sight of the LORD. They forgot the LORD their God, and served the Baals and Asherahs. Therefore the anger of the LORD was hot against Israel, and He sold them into the hand of Cushan-Rishathaim king of Mesopotamia; and the children of Israel served Cushan-Rishathaim eight years. When the children of Israel cried out to the LORD, the LORD raised up a *deliverer* for the children of Israel, who *delivered* them" (Judg. 3:7-9). A biblical judge *delivers*.

We have learned that a biblical judge *decides, delivers, teaches,* and *rules.* After *deciding* who is innocent, he *delivers* the innocent from the guilty. He doesn't just sit behind a bench making decisions. He actively comes down and delivers the innocent from the guilty.

In reality each person passes judgment on himself/ herself by his/her actions (deeds). Christ simply ratifies and pronounces the final decision based on the evidence of a person's deeds. For example, the Israelites passed judgment on themselves by whether or not they put blood on the doorpost the night of the exodus. By that evidence God could see who was obedient. He then delivered the obedient and ruled over them, teaching them as He led them across the desert to Mt. Sinai where He gave them His covenant.

From heaven Christ was doing the work of a biblical judge when He *decided* the time had come to deliver His people so He sent Moses to *deliver* His people from Egypt. He then served as their leader/*ruler* as He, in a pillar of fire and cloud, took them to Mt. Sinai where He *taught* them His covenant and more by inspiring the first five books of the Bible, the Torah or Pentateuch.

In the U.S. we have a legislative branch, the House of Representatives and the Senate, that passes laws and makes them known, or teaches, them to the nation. We have the executive branch, the president, who is responsible for ruling and enforcing the laws, and we have a judicial branch that decided the legality of laws according to precedent and the Constitution, and the guilt or innocence of cases brought to it (decides, delivers, sets free the innocent).

Biblical judges also perform all four of these functions. Therefore, Christ performs all four. Christ is our Lord *(rules)*. Christ has given us His laws *(teaches)*. Christ investigates the record of our lives *(decides)*. And Christ is even now working to *deliver* His people in His own special way.

If we love the Lord Jesus Christ, we will *want* to be judged by Him, which entails willingly living by His decisions and being ruled by Him, taught by Him, and delivered by Him, for He is all merciful. "He has not dealt with us according to our sins, Nor punished us according to our iniquities. For as the heavens are high above the earth, So great is His mercy toward those who fear Him; As far as the east is from the west, So far has He removed our transgressions from us. As a father pities his children, So the LORD pities those who fear Him. For He knows our frame; He remembers that we are dust" (Ps. 103:10-14).

God is on our side. He wants to judge us, teach us, deliver us, and decide in our favor. He wants to save us. All these functions are necessary and in operation during the investigative judgment in order for God to take the kingdom from the little horn and give it to the saints.

Chapter 5

"Judge Me Please"

If the judgment is good news, is it good news to you? Do you want to be judged? If the judgment were to proceed to the cases of the living right now, would you want to be judged right now? That may depend on your understanding of the investigative judgment. Let's hear the word of the saints in the Bible.

What does David say in Psalm 7:8? "Judge me, O LORD, according to my righteousness, and according to my integrity within me." So why does David want to be judged? Because he knows what it means to be judged by our Lord. Notice how he begins Psalm 7. "O LORD my God, in You I put my trust; *Save* me from all those who persecute me; and *deliver* me" (verse 1). Save me, deliver me, judge me. All three words are bundled together and have essentially the same meaning. To judge me, if I am righteous, is to deliver me, which is to save me. When David is asking God to judge him, he is asking God to deliver him or save him.

The children of Israel repeatedly engaged in wicked activities and were often sold into the hands of their enemies. When they would cry out to the Lord, they were essentially crying out to be judged. In response to their cry, the Lord raised up judges to deliver them. I know we don't usually think this way about judging and delivering, but we must learn to think in biblical terms.

Now read carefully the following verses in the King James Version, (KJV), and compare them with the New King James Version (NKJV). They read differently, but you immediately see what the word "judge" implies.

- "Judge me, O LORD; for I have walked in mine integrity" (Ps. 26:1, KJV).
- "Vindicate me, O LORD, for I have walked in my integrity" (Ps. 26:1, NKJV).

- "Judge me, O LORD my God, according to thy righteousness" (Ps. 35:24, KJV).
- "Vindicate me, O LORD my God, according to Your righteousness" (Ps. 35:24, NKJV).

- "Judge me, O God, and plead my cause against an ungodly nation: O *deliver* me from the deceitful and unjust man" (Ps. 43:1, KJV).
- "Vindicate me, O God, and plead my cause against an ungodly nation: Oh, *deliver* me from the deceitful and unjust man!" (Ps. 43:1, NKJV).

In the NKJV the Hebrew (and Greek in the Septuagint) word translated "vindicate" in the above verses is translated "judge" in Psalm 7:8: "Judge me O Lord, according to my righteousness...." The word for judge is translated consistently, and more accurately in my mind, as when it remains "judge" as in the KJV. Translators of the NKJV took the liberty of *interpreting* the word rather than *translating* it.

Vindicate *is one* of the things that happens to the righteous in the judgment, but it is only *one* thing. By using the word "vindicate" instead of "judge," the reader sees only one part of what judging accomplishes, and one part of what David wants. David wants deliverance. So by failing to translate the word as "judge," the reader is not able to see that David wants more than vindication. He *wants* to be judged. To be *judged* is something to be desired, cherished, and yearned for, because it means to be delivered or saved. There's more.

Hebrew Poetry

The psalms are written in Hebrew poetry. Various poetic structures are used in Hebrew poetry, one of which is parallels that "rhyme" thoughts rather than sounds as we often do in English. We like to rhyme the sounds of words:

> Mary had a little lamb.
> whose fleece was white as snow.
> And everywhere that Mary went,
> the lamb was sure to go.

"Go" rhymes with "snow." Bravo! But Hebrew parallelisms are much grander in my view because of how they "rhyme" thoughts. A parallelism is where a word in one line expresses the same thought as a different word in a parallel line. We can learn a great deal about the meanings or definitions of words by these parallelisms.

Look again to see the parallel in Psalm 43:1 above. Here is the structure: a' is parallel to a, and b' is parallel to b.

a) "Judge me, O God, and plead my cause against"
b) "an ungodly nation"

a') "O deliver me from"
b') "the deceitful and unjust man"

In the KJV the word "deliver" is parallel to "judge." Notice also that to "plead my cause" reinforces the word "judge" so that to judge means to plead David's cause as well as to deliver him. By this parallel we see the same meaning for judge as we did in the last chapter—to judge is to deliver. The rest of the verse is in parallel form also. An "ungodly nation" is parallel to the "deceitful and unjust man." The latter may refer to the man who is king of an ungodly nation.

Psalm 43:1 is only one of many passages where to *judge* means to *deliver*, so you can see why the righteous long to be judged and why the judgment-hour message is the good news of the everlasting gospel. Now let's contemplate a few additional texts. Not all of them are examples of parallelisms, and not all of them use the word deliver, but you can see that deliverance is what happens to the righteous as a result of God's judgment.

Notice also what happens to the wicked as a result of God's judgment. He delivers one and destroys another. That's what a biblical judge does.

Oh, let the wickedness of the wicked come to

an end. But establish the just; for the righteous God tests the hearts and minds. My defense is of God, who saves the upright in heart. God is a just judge, and God is angry with the wicked every day (Ps. 7:9-11).

When God arose to judgment, to deliver all the oppressed of the earth (Ps, 76:9).

I will bear the indignation of the LORD, because I have sinned against Him, until He *pleads my case and executes justice* for me.... Then she who is my enemy will see, and shame will cover her who said to me, 'Where is the LORD your God?' My eyes will see her; now she will be trampled down like mud in the streets (Mic. 7:9, 10).

With righteousness He shall judge the poor, and decide with equity for the meek of the earth; He shall strike the earth with the rod of His mouth, and with the breath of His lips He shall slay the wicked (Isa. 11:4).

Look again at Psalm 26:1-3, and use the word *judge* in place of *vindicate*. The parallelisms are compounded, but still easy to see. Don't let the verse division trick you. They were put in by man and can mask some of these parallels.

Judge me, O LORD, for I have walked in my integrity. I have also trusted in the LORD; I shall not slip. Examine me, O Lord, and prove me; try my mind and my heart. For Your lovingkindness is before my eyes, and I have walked in Your truth.

"Judge me" and "examine me" are in parallel. To judge is to examine. But after "examine me" are redundancies such as "prove me," "try my mind," "test me" (marginal reading). We saw the same activity earlier in Psalm 7:8, 9. After David says, "Judge me, O LORD, according to my righteousness, and according to my integrity within me," he says, "Oh, let the wickedness of the wicked come to an end, but *establish* the just; for the righteous God *tests* the hearts and minds." So to judge is more than looking over past records and making a decision. It is testing and proving while we are still living.

Wow! We just said something very important about the investigative judgment and why it takes so long. Judgment is not just looking over the past records, but it is a *process* of testing and proving while we are still living. Why would God prove people since He already knows their hearts except to establish them, secure them, and show to other interested watchers in the universe His righteous judgment?

God's followers are on display to the onlooking universes as they respond to the situations of life. These situations become His tests through which they pass judgment on themselves. Those who pass He saves. Those who fail either destroy themselves or will be put out of their misery in the end.

Incidentally, if you are bothered by David's asking to be judged according to *his* righteousness, when you know David did many things that were not righteous, it is because David is not viewing his righteousness according to a moral standard as we do but according to his singular relationship to Jehovah. David did not go astray to worship other gods like Solomon and others. His heart was set on Him whom we call the Lord. So whether his moral behavior was up or down according to our way of measuring morality, he always turned to the Lord, not to Baal or other false gods. In this he was righteous, faithful, true.

Christ Our Deliverer

Let's come back to Christ as our deliverer. A biblical judge delivers his people from their enemies. Although political powers and economic competitors and tyrannical religions can be satanically inspired, threatening our freedoms, our livelihood, and even life itself, nevertheless, our greatest enemies on earth are not national or political or economic powers. "We do not wrestle against flesh and blood" (Eph. 6:12). Our greatest enemies are the same as they were for Jesus: the second death, religious bigotry, false teachings, and Satan himself. Paul wrote, "The last enemy that will be destroyed is death" (1 Cor. 15:26). Death is an enemy. There should be no question that Satan and his falsehoods are enemies. But Christ will deliver us from all of them if we are willing.

Beginning in 1844 the greatest enemies the church faced at that time in the history of the great controversy were the strangleholds the major religions of the world had and still have on their governments and people, and especially the false doctrines of the papacy that are further embraced and enforced by the Protestant world, some of which are responsible for creating modern secularism and atheism.

I will mention a few, but I will not elaborate on the

effect of the papacy's false teachings and its demoralizing affect on Protestantism and society. Books have been written documenting its bloodshed and corruptions. Following is a list of some of the false teachings that God's righteous people must shun:

- Celibacy of the clergy, which has led to enormous immorality among priests and nuns.
- The veneration of images (idols) and relics contrary to the second commandment.
- The sainting and invocation of dead priests and nuns, implying that they are alive instead of dead.
- The veneration and invocation of Mary leading to miracles of spiritualism.
- The sale of indulgences, which has made the Vatican one of the richest institutions in the world. According to Roman Catholic teaching, an indulgence is the remission of part or all of the temporal and especially purgatorial punishment that is due for sins whose eternal punishment has been remitted and whose guilt has been pardoned (as through the sacrament of penance).
- Immortality of the soul.
- The doctrine that God punishes people in an eternally burning hell.
- The doctrine of purgatory from which souls must be paid for and prayed out of.
- The infallibility of the popes.
- That a human priest can forgive confessed sins.
- The church's denunciation of the separation of church and state.

- Sunday sacredness.

By examining the corruptions between church and state and their coercive influence on society found in Revelation 13 and 17, in order for God's people to *overcome,* they must come out of Babylon and remain true to the peculiar doctrines of the true church.

If you read carefully the promises to those who overcome in the seven churches of Revelation, you will find that overcoming is not so much overcoming personal sin and practicing personal piety as it is breaking free from, or overcoming, the overwhelming social, economic, and political pressures of the false religious world and remaining true to God. Those pressures will be some of the worst the world has ever seen because it is Satan's last effort to defeat the remnant church. I can't imagine them being worse than the inquisition, but the dire warnings against those who receive the mark of the beast is in proportion to the atrocities the beast and its image will do to the saints. I do not mean to diminish the need for personal morality, especially as magnified by Paul, but rather to properly represent what is most important for salvation as emphasized throughout Scripture.

Christ longs to deliver us and fight our battles for us, but we must first sincerely request His help. All heaven is poised to rescue both adults and children when they truly cry out to be delivered from the corruptions of this present age. At this time more than any other in earth's history, during the investigative judgment, being true to Him is essential to God's plan of restoration. Keeping us true is Christ's work in the heavenly sanctuary.

Chapter 6

The Hour of His Deliverance Has Come

In chapter 3 we learned that the first angel's message in Revelation 14:7, "The hour of His judgment has come," is good news, and it is good news because the investigative judgment takes the dominion away from the little horn of Daniel 7 and gives it to the saints of the Most High. In chapter 4 we learned that a judge teaches, rules, decides cases, and especially *delivers* the innocent from the guilty, or the righteous from the wicked. And in chapter 5 we learned that the saints want to be judged because to be judged means to be delivered.

Notice how the saints under the altar in Revelation 6:9, during the fifth seal, cry out longingly for God to judge, "How long, O Lord, holy and true, until You judge and avenge our blood on those who dwell on the earth?" (verse 10). From what we have learned, we should know that when the saints are asking God to judge and avenge their blood, they are simply asking God to put an end to human suffering and be delivered, in this case from death, for biblical judgment always bears this two-edged sword of delivering the righteous and punishing the wicked.

In this chapter we will learn how God is delivering His people *during* the investigative judgment and what He did in 1844 to begin judging—i.e. *teaching, delivering and ruling*—His people.

First, consider this question. What do most people want to be delivered from?

- *Disease,* with its pain, suffering, fear of death, costliness.
- *Poverty,* with its inability to own nice things, travel, and buy for their children.
- *Slavery,* whether by men, or women, or addictions, or another nation.
- *Sin* itself, with its guilt, fear, insecurity, loss of heaven.
- *Temptation,* with its power to lure and deceive.
- *Prison,* with its restrictions of freedom, and often harsh conditions, embarrassment, loss of friends, position, and self-esteem.
- *Anger,* rage, resentment, and jealousy that breeds hatred and division.
- *Ignorance,* in most cases, individually and as a nation, we would rather know than not know.
- *Wickedness,* from both the wicked and their degrading, corrupting ways of life.
- *Death* itself.

Now let's see how God delivers from any and all of the above and much more. Diseases will get worse and worse in the last days, but we do not need to fear if we know and keep His commandments, statutes, and judgments (Deut. 7:11-15).

It is a four-step process:

1. His commandments must be *revealed by inspiration* to His people,
2. as individuals, we *learn* His commandments,
3. then we *do* His commandments,
4. and God keeps His side of the agreement (covenant) and blesses us. When we do our best, God does the rest. Thus, we are delivered from those diseases.

Now watch how these four steps are found in Deuteronomy: "Surely I have taught you statutes and judgments, just as the LORD my God commanded me, that you should act according to them ... Therefore be careful to observe them" (Deut. 4:5, 6). "Therefore you shall keep the commandment, the statutes, and the judgments which I command you today, to observe them. Then it shall come to pass, because you listen to these judgments, and keep and do them, that the LORD your God will keep with you the covenant and the mercy which He swore to your fathers. And He will love you and bless you ... And the LORD will take away from you all sickness" (Deut. 7:11-15).

God has shown us how to be delivered from more than 90-plus percent of the diseases of the world. How? By revelation! By revealing His health secrets in the Bible and the writings of Ellen G. White. We learn His health secrets by reading or listening, but we must obey what He has revealed if we are to be delivered from disease. If we do our best, God will do the rest. Ninety percent is not an exaggeration. The World Health Organization tells us that 90 percent of the diseases from which men suffer could be prevented by lifestyle changes. Most of us choose the way we die by the way we choose to live.

Poverty is a relative term depending on which country you live in. Nevertheless God has provided a remedy.

> Then it shall come to pass, because you listen to these judgments, and keep and do them, that the LORD your God will keep with you the covenant and the mercy which He swore to your fathers. And He will love you and bless you and multiply you; He will also bless the fruit of your womb and the fruit of you land, your grain and your new wine and your oil, the increase of your cattle and the offspring of your flock ... You shall be blessed above all peoples (Deut. 7:12-14).

> Do not mix with the winebibbers, or with gluttonous eaters of meat; For the drunkard and the glutton will come to poverty, and drowsiness will clothe a man with rags (Prov. 23:20, 21).

> Go to the ant, you sluggard! Consider her ways and be wise, which, having no captain, overseer or ruler, provides her supplies in the summer, and gathers her food in the harvest. How long will you slumber, O sluggard? When will you rise from your sleep? A little sleep, a little slumber, a little folding of the hands to sleep—So shall your poverty come on you like a prowler, and your need like an armed man (Prov. 6:6-11).

"Bring all the tithes into the storehouse, that there may be food in My house, and try Me now in this," says the Lord of hosts, "If I will not open for you the windows of heaven and pour out for you such blessing that there will not be room enough to receive it. And I will rebuke the devourer for your sakes, so that he will not destroy the fruit of your ground, nor shall the vine fail to bear fruit for you in the field," Says the LORD of hosts (Mal. 3:10, 11).

How does God deliver us from poverty? By revealing the success secrets of life, by learning those secrets, and then by obeying them, He will guarantee our prosperity, great or small, but nevertheless, secure. God does not promise that we will be millionaires, but He does promise that our bread and water will be sure.

By now, you see the formula. It is really quite simple. God reveals truth. We learn truth. We obey truth. Then with His help we are delivered from the bondage of error through truths He has revealed. The same is true for the following and a lot more.

God counsels us on how to avoid slavery to alcohol (Prov. 23:31); sex (Prov. 7); drugs; riches (Prov. 23:4); power, position, and prestige (Matt. 23:6; Mark 12:39; Luke 11:43, 20:46); or appetite (Prov. 23:2). Peter gives us the assurance in 2 Peter 2:9 that "the Lord knows how to deliver the godly out of temptations," such as those that enslave us and many more.

Many people long to be delivered from anger and the power it can hold upon them. They long to be peacemakers as God desires: "Blessed are the peacemakers, for they shall be called the sons of God" (Matt. 5:9; see also Ps. 37 and Heb. 12:14, 15).

As followers of God, we also long to be delivered from ignorance; we long to understand God's Word and His law (Ps. 119:97-104). But above all, we long to be delivered from sin itself and the fear of death (Ps. 119:9-11; Heb. 2:15).

Remember the mixed multitude from Egypt? They wanted to be delivered from Egyptian bondage, but they didn't want to be delivered from the flesh pots of Egypt, and they didn't want to adopt God's ways of living in the wilderness. They wanted to grab the Promised Land with one hand and hold on to Egypt with the other. So God let them die in the wilderness.

> Moreover, brethren, I do not want you to be unaware that all our fathers were under the cloud, all passed through the sea, all were baptized into Moses in the cloud and in the sea, all ate the same spiritual food, and all drank the same spiritual drink. For they drank of the spiritual Rock that followed them, and that Rock was Christ. But with most of them God was not well pleased, for their bodies were scattered in the wilderness. Now these things became our examples, to the intent that we should not lust after evil things as they also lusted (1 Cor. 10:1-6).

They were delivered only part way. They were delivered from Egypt, but they weren't delivered from their own lusts, so they didn't get into the Promised Land. Apparently we have some growing to do after we are baptized.

So do you want to be delivered now? Or do you want to suffer in ignorance and disobedience but hope to be delivered from death at the resurrection? Please listen. The only ones who will be delivered when Jesus returns are those who strive to be delivered from Egyptian bondage *now*.

> The way of return can be gained only by hard fighting, inch by inch, every hour. By a momentary act of will, one may place himself in the power of evil; but it requires more than a momentary act of will to break these fetters and attain to a higher, holier life. The purpose may be formed, the work begun; but its accomplishment will require toil, time, and perseverance, patience and sacrifice.... No one will be borne upward without stern, persevering effort in his own behalf. All must engage in this warfare for themselves. Individually we are responsible for the issue of the struggle (*Testimonies for the Church,* vol. 8, pp. 313, 314).

So do you really want to be delivered? It's a fair question because of our ambivalence. I am writing as if *you really* want deliverance, and for the sake of *others who really* want deliverance.

Delivering the Remnant

When the investigative judgment began in 1844, what did God do from the heavenly sanctuary to *deliver* His people from the things listed above and many more?

Before you answer, consider this: whenever God

makes a major move in the sanctuary, He pours light upon His people.

At the very time God said, "Let them make Me a sanctuary [the *earthly* sanctuary], that I may dwell among them," (Exod. 25:8), the Lord said to Moses, "Write these words, for according to the tenor of these words I have made a covenant with you and with Israel" (Exod. 34:27). When God told Moses to build the sanctuary, He also told Moses to write. Moses wrote, and a *flood of inspired light* came to us through the first five books (scrolls) of the Bible—the Pentateuch, the law, the Torah—that formed the beginning of the Old Testament. It was God's idea to give us His Word (scrolls) to teach His people.

When Jesus inaugurated the *heavenly* sanctuary "with His own blood" (Heb. 9:12), He, at the same time, gave us a *flood of inspired light* through the Holy Spirit and the New Testament as He promised when He was here. "The Holy Spirit, whom the Father will send in My name, He will teach you all things, and bring to your remembrance all things that I said to you" (John 14:26). We wouldn't know about Jesus were it not for the New Testament.

In 1844, the very same year Jesus moved into the *second* apartment of the *heavenly* sanctuary, He opened a *flood of inspired light* through "the testimony of Jesus," the Spirit of Prophecy, otherwise known as the writings of Ellen G. White.

So what happened in 1844? Something very big! The remnant church received a spiritual gift in what we call the Spirit of Prophecy. The writings of Mrs. White are a phenomenon in the world of inspired writings. Never has there been such a prolific writer of truth in the ages of human history. So never believe people who say, "Nothing happened in 1844," for we have in our hands something visible and tangible, a "spiritual gift" from heaven as evidence that Christ made a major move in the heavenly sanctuary. Her inspired writings tell us what move Christ made and why. That's not circular reasoning because we have ample, ample evidence that Ellen White was an inspired messenger, and when an inspired messenger speaks, God's people can believe. Thus, from the study of Bible prophecy and the enlightened writings of Ellen White, the investigative judgment began in 1844.

Out of His great love for us, God delivers His people by giving us light. Out of our love for Him, we then learn from that light and act upon it. God then delivers as we act on the light He has given. The following stories are examples of God's providence and the revelation of new light:

> Jesus gave advance military intelligence to the Christians who obeyed Him in the apostolic times. "When you see Jerusalem surrounded by armies, then know that its desolation is near. Then let those who are in Judea flee to the mountains, let those who are in the midst of her depart, and let not those who are in the country enter her" (Luke 21:20, 21). No Christian died in Jerusalem when it was destroyed in AD 70 because the Christians obeyed Christ and fled Jerusalem in AD 66. So the Christians were *delivered* from death and/or captivity by following His Word and obeying the light given to them.

73

During World War II churches were outlawed by one European country. Some of our Adventist brethren went to the Ministry of the Interior and explained that Seventh-day Adventists were not a political group and that they obeyed the laws of the government. The minister was inclined to exempt Adventists, but the ruling had already been made against all churches. But the minister himself suggested, "Why don't you call yourselves 'Bible Searchers' rather than a church, so then you can continue to meet." Our brethren readily and gleefully accepted his suggestion. "Yes! 'Bible Searchers.' That's what we are."

The word went out. But the word went faster by the church's tell-an-Adventist than by the government's tel-e-graph, so some of our believers began to meet before government officials got the word, and they were arrested and imprisoned. Eventually, leading brethren from the church's headquarters arrived with papers from the Ministry of the Interior to release Seventh-day Adventists from captivity.

The commandant of the prison and the president of the union supervised while another church officer began reading the names of the Adventists. All whose names were read were lined up in front of the commandant who then told them they were free to go. When the other prisoners heard their release, a man in the yard yelled, "I'm an Adventist." The Adventists turned to look and said, "Yes, he's an

Adventist." The officer looked at his list and shook his head saying, "No, your name is not here." Another yelled, "I'm an Adventist." Again the small group in front turned and said, "Yes, he's an Adventist." Again the officer looked at his book and shook his head. The scene was repeated until all whose names were in the book were released. From what book was the officer reading? The church treasurer's records! Only those who had given tithes and offerings had their names recorded in the book. The true Adventists were *delivered* by their obedience.

Seventh-day Adventists have long had advance information on the causes and prevention of disease. "All our enjoyment or suffering may be traced to obedience or transgression of natural law.... To make plain natural law, and urge the obedience of it, is the work that accompanies the third angel's message, to prepare a people for the coming of the Lord" (*Counsels on Diet and Foods,* p. 69). Our suffering to a certain degree comes from what Adam and his descendents did or failed to do.

Seventh-day Adventists have advance information on Christian perfection in connection with our health. "It is impossible for those who indulge the appetite to attain to Christian perfection" (Ibid., p. 22). "God requires of His people continual advancement. We need to learn that indulged appetite is the greatest hindrance to mental improvement and soul sanctification" (Ibid., p. 45). Furthermore, "Nine tenths of the wickedness among the children of today is caused by intemperance in eating and drinking" (*Temperance,* p. 150).

If we want to be delivered from disease and wickedness, we *must* obey the laws of health. God gave *much* light on this subject because the connection of body, mind, and soul is so inseparable.

I have not yet made clear how God's inspired writings *rule* us. It is easy to see how they *teach* us and *deliver* us. And we can see how we are *judged* (redundancy noted) by them. But how do they *rule* us? The United States is governed by the "rule of law," by its Constitution and local ordinances, in contrast to rule by a single person, be they a benevolent or malevolent dictator or king. Citizens living under the rule of law are expected to understand its principles, embrace its philosophy, obey its laws, and be judged by them in a court of law.

Likewise, God has given us a comprehensive philosophy in the great controversy being played out on earth. He has revealed His character and His law. He has stated and illustrated His principles at work in the universe. And He gives us rules to live by. To willingly submit to God is to willingly submit to *rule* by law revealed in His Word. We are guided and governed by law, and we will be judged by law. We are held accountable for a knowledge of His laws, including the knowledge of His laws we might have known had we not been too lazy or too busy with the cares of this life to learn and obey them.

The god of this world is binding his subjects into bundles to be burned. God's way of delivering His people from getting bundled into the wrong bundle is by bathing them with light, with true knowledge/wisdom. Just before reproving the Galatians for embracing error, Paul wrote, "Grace to you and peace from God the Father and our Lord Jesus Christ, who gave Himself for our sins, that He might *deliver us from this present evil age*, according to the will of our God and Father" (Gal. 1:3, 4). Delivering "us from this present evil age" does not refer to being delivered from planet earth at His second coming as much as it does to being delivered *now* from the power and practice of sin which is so destructive.

So when the first angel's message was first preached in 1844, "Fear God and give glory to Him, for the hour of His judgment [the hour of His deliverance] has come," little did the speaker realize how much was contained in the judgment-hour message, for in that very year God began sending forth seventy years of messages to teach, to rule, to test, and to deliver His people (Rev. 14:7).

Those messages came directly from the second apartment of the heavenly sanctuary. There is so much more to the investigative judgment and the sanctuary message than we have realized. It is a process at this particular time in the plan of restoration of extracting and purifying His people that is necessary to prepare His people to stand and take the kingdom from the little horn and give it to the saints.

The first beast of Revelation 13, which is the same

papal power as the little horn, had 1260 years to display its nature and rule. It received a deadly wound in 1798, made possible by the rediscovery of the Word that had been eclipsed by papal tradition. Now Christ makes His move into the Most Holy Place and brings out the true church from 1260 years underground, to display its nature by restoring the law of God with special emphasis on the Sabbath, the seal of God.

Showing the contrast between these two powers, the harlot of Revelation 17 and the pure woman of Revelation 12, is essential to justifying the sanctuary and closing the plan of redemption.

Chapter 7

Atonement Is a Big Word

From time to time I have mused over questions like, "What is so important about the second apartment ministry? And why is there a judgment when God already knows who are His and who are not?" People have also asked me, "What has Christ been doing in the first apartment for the last 1800 years? Is His first apartment ministry still continuing while He is in the second apartment?"

The Investigative Judgment in the Day of Atonement

In Adventist theology we view the investigative judgment as part of the antitypical day of atonement in the heavenly sanctuary. In the earthly sanctuary services, once a year the high priest entered the Most Holy Place on the Day of Atonement, at which time the sins that had been transferred to the sanctuary throughout the year were removed from the sanctuary. On that day the people of God were to "afflict their souls," repent of any wrongs they were harboring. On that day both the sanctuary and the people were symbolically *cleansed*—the sins of God's people were removed from the camp, *never to return*.

As Adventists, we view the cleansing of the heavenly sanctuary and the cleansing of God's people on earth as the antitypical, the real day of atonement, the day in which we are now living. But the heavenly sanctuary cannot be *cleansed*, i.e. the sins cannot be removed, until the records of all professed believers have been investigated and decided upon, hence the name, investigative judgment. But the sanctuary cannot be cleansed until the last generation is ready for translation. That process started in 1844 and is still going on.

The investigative judgment takes a long time because it is more than going over records. It includes a process of testing, perfecting, and proving the last generation of saints on earth. This work is prefigured in Malachi 3:3: "He will sit as a refiner and a purifier of silver; He will purify the sons of Levi, and purge them as gold and silver, that they may offer to the LORD an offering in righteousness."

If you read further in Malachi 3, you will see that after God has purified the righteous He will punish the wicked. But first He must demonstrate to a watching universe that He has the *right*, that He is *just*, to punish the wicked. He has already gained that right as a result of Christ's perfection. But He must do more by perfecting the 144,000. (We will examine that further in the next chapter.) Gaining that right is one reason I keep quoting the following statement:

> The intercession of Christ in man's behalf in the sanctuary above is as essential to the plan of salvation as was His death upon the cross. By His death He began that work which after

His resurrection He ascended to complete in heaven (*The Great Controversy*, p. 489).

In the final stages of Christ's second-apartment ministry, cleansing the heavenly sanctuary and cleansing the remnant people in the church are virtually synonymous. So along with *deciding* who has remained true to Him and who has not, He is working intensely (but patiently) to bring His people, His church, to maturity, to perfection, not sinlessness, but total commitment. So I may often use interchangeably the terms, investigative judgment, Christ's intercession in the heavenly sanctuary, and the day of atonement, even though the day of atonement extends beyond the other two. In the next chapter I hope to make clear *why*. Why this work in man's behalf *at this particular time* is essential to God's plan of salvation.

Incidentally, knowing that Christ's intercession in the Most Holy Place is *part* of the atonement should have resolved the unfortunate debate about whether or not the atonement was complete(d) on the cross. The atoning sacrifice of Christ on the cross was definitely complete if by *complete* is meant *adequate* to satisfy the claims of the law, to provide a *vicarious* atonement, and to satisfy the angels, but the "atonement" as the word is used in the Bible was not completed on the cross. The atonement will not be completed until sin, sinners, and Satan are destroyed. So let's examine the word atonement as used in the Bible.

Understanding Atonement

When Christians use the word atonement, they usually

think only of Christ's death on the cross. His death on the cross is central and absolutely essential to the atonement and to our salvation. But Christ's death on the cross was God's *vicarious* atonement, His substitutionary death, His dying the second death in our place and making satisfaction for our sins. But Christ's death is only one part of the atonement. There are several parts. Before His death He lived a perfect life. Remember how the sacrificial lamb had to be without blemish because it represented Christ's life, which was without blemish. If Jesus had not lived a perfect life for thirty-three years, which is much harder to do than dying, then His death would not have been adequate to make an atonement for sin. So His perfect life was an essential part of the atonement also. But there is still more.

Throughout the year priests accepted the sacrifices and offerings brought to the sanctuary by individuals. The priest administered the blood upon the altar in a prescribed manner, which transferred the sins from the person to the sanctuary, making an atonement for the individual (Lev. 1-23). So "atonement" was going on all year long. This daily round of services, including the daily or morning and evening sacrifices, represented the work Christ has been doing in the heavenly sanctuary since His ascension, and ever since Adam fell for that matter, but we won't get side tracked right now.

Then came the annual Day of Atonement when the high priest entered the Most Holy Place first for himself and his family and second for the assembly of God's people. The annual ceremony represented the closing ministry of Christ in the Most Holy Place of the heavenly sanctuary, which began in 1844.

That atonement ceremony also depicted the final eradication of sin and sinners. In the Day of Atonement service, two goats were presented before the Lord: "Then Aaron shall cast lots for the two goats: one lot for the LORD and the other lot for the scapegoat" (Lev. 16:8). The goat on which the "lot for the Lord" fell represented Jesus Christ. That goat was then slain, and its blood was brought into the sanctuary with which "he [Aaron] shall make *atonement* for the Holy Place, because of the uncleanness of the children of Israel, and because of their transgressions, for all their sins ... for all the assembly of Israel" (verses 16, 17).

Christ died 2,000 years ago, so obviously the atonement was not finished at the death of the Lord's goat or at the death of Christ because the next step was to bring the blood into the Most Holy Place with which he shall make an *atonement,* i.e. *cleanse* the sanctuary and the people. So there is more to atonement than the death of the Lamb. Christ's work in the Most Holy Place, which began 1800 years after His death, is part of *the atonement*. But even when He has finished His intercessory work in the Most Holy Place, the *atonement* is still not finished.

Leviticus 16:20 reads, "When he has *made an end of atoning* for the Holy Place ... he shall bring the live goat [representing Satan] ... [and] confess over it all the iniquities of the children of Israel." Then it is sent away *alive* into the wilderness. At the risk of saying something twice, when the high priest "has made an end of atoning for the Holy Place [and for the people]," that's all he has done so far is make an atonement for the Holy Place and for the whole assembly, but the work of atonement is not yet finished. Look at Leviticus 16:10: "The goat on which the lot fell to be the scapegoat shall be presented alive before the LORD, to make *atonement* upon it, and to let it go as the scapegoat into the wilderness."

The scapegoat was not slain for the sins of the people as was the Lord's goat. It was not slain by the priest, and it was certainly not slain as a vicarious sacrifice. Instead, it was led *alive* into the wilderness, representing Satan's banishment to the desolate earth during the millennium. The scapegoat was probably torn apart by wolves, which would be a fitting symbol of the wicked turning on Satan at the close of the millennium. Although the earthly Day of Atonement ceremony didn't take us that far, it is easily conjectured.

In harmony with the principle, "Whatever a man sows [angels too], that he will also reap," the sins for which Satan is responsible and for which Christ died are eventually rolled back on Satan, the scapegoat. Let's examine Leviticus 16:20, 21 one more time: "When he [Aaron] has made an end of atoning for the Holy Place, the tabernacle of meeting, and the altar, he shall bring the live goat. Aaron shall lay both his hands on the head of the live goat, confess over it all the iniquities of the children of Israel, and all their transgressions, concerning all their sins, putting them on the head of the goat, and shall send it away into the wilderness."

Don't be misled by the word *confess*, as if it meant

confessing sins to God. It didn't. It has no relation to going to confession. Confessing here was simply *pronouncing* the sins that the high priest brought out from the sanctuary and transferring them to the scapegoat by laying his hands on the scapegoat and making this pronouncement.

The scapegoat represents Satan. Placing the sins from the sanctuary on the head of the scapegoat is part of the *atonement*. That is why atonement is sometimes referred to as "at-one-ment," a time when we are *one with God* with nothing sinful between us. Sin is forever removed from the saints. So, biblically the *atonement,* the at-one-ment, is not completed until Satan, sin, and sinners are no more, and there is complete harmony in the universes among God and His people and the angels.

> In the ministration of the tabernacle, and of the temple that afterward took its place, the people were taught each day, by means of types and shadows, the great truths relative to the advent of Christ as Redeemer, Priest, and King; and once each year their minds were carried forward to the closing events of the great controversy between Christ and Satan, the final purification of the universe from sin and sinners (*Prophets and Kings,* pp. 684, 685).

We will see later that one of the things Christ is doing in the investigative judgment is giving God the right to destroy Satan and all who cling to him. As a result of that judgment, both the righteous and eventually the wicked will bow. "Every knee shall bow to Me, and every tongue shall confess to God" (Rom. 14:11). "At the name of Jesus every knee should bow, of those in heaven, and of those on earth, and of those under the earth" (Phil. 2:10).

Hopefully we have enlarged our understanding of the scope of the atonement, just as we enlarged our understanding of the everlasting gospel. In fact, the atonement and everlasting gospel are close to synonymous. They both refer to the time when:

> The great controversy is ended. Sin and sinners are no more. The entire universe is clean. One pulse of harmony and gladness beats through the vast creation. From Him who created all, flow life and light and gladness, throughout the realms of illimitable space. From the minutest atom to the greatest world, all things, animate and inanimate, in their unshadowed beauty and perfect joy, declare that God is love (*The Great Controversy*, p. 678).

However, if you want to tantalize your imagination a little with who paid the ransom for our redemption, check out Deuteronomy 32:6, Psalm 74:2, Isaiah 43:1-3, Proverbs 21:18.

Chapter 8

An Essential Ministry

Let's ask the question again, "Why did Christ give us special revelation in the writings of Ellen White *at this particular time*?" Yes, I know they were to bring us back to the Bible, to help us understand the Bible, and to help us apply the Bible, but why at this particular time in the plan of salvation? God wouldn't do that unless it was necessary. Why is it so necessary *now* as compared to AD 1516 or 1744 or … ?

Just as "the earth was dark through misapprehension of God" (*The Desire of Ages*, p. 22) when Jesus first came to lift the gloomy shadows, so the earth was darkened again during the Middle Ages and needs to be "illuminated with his glory" (Rev. 18:1).

Select portions of Ellen White's writings tell us that Christ is going over the names of all the professed believers in the investigative judgment. But most of her writings have to do with practical godliness; in fact, she often writes about superlative practical godliness, as if more is expected of us than of those in past millenniums. But why did God give us her counsel at this particular time in history, writings designed to bring us to a much higher level of Christianity than was required of Martin Luther or

87

Carl Zwingli or John Wesley? Is that more important now than 600 years ago, and if so, *why*?

This quote was presented earlier, but it answers this question. "It is the unbelief, the worldliness, unconsecration, and strife among the Lord's professed people that have kept us in this world of sin and sorrow so many years" (*Selected Messages,* book 1, p. 69). Apparently the condition of the Lord's professed people has something to do with the timing of Christ's second coming. Is the condition of Christ's professed people on earth changed by His work in the sanctuary ministry? Or does He simply make a decision at the end whether we made it or not? Regarding the last question, we have already learned that a biblical judge is not passive but very active in delivering the righteous from the wicked and that one of His ways of delivering the remnant is by enlightening them, giving them *a flood of inspired light,* which corresponds with the inspired information Ellen White began sharing in 1844.

I must quote again a passage from *The Great Controversy,* for this statement and the material in this chapter are my reasons for writing this book. "The intercession of Christ in man's behalf in the sanctuary above is as essential to the plan of salvation as His death on the cross. By His death He began that work which after His resurrection He ascended to complete in heaven" (p. 489).

The context of this statement shows that the intercession of Christ referred to here is not so much His work in the first apartment, which began 1800 years ago, 6000-plus really, and still continues, but it refers to His work in the second apartment, the Most Holy Place.

"The subject of the sanctuary and the investigative judgment should be clearly understood by the people of God. All need a knowledge for themselves of the position and work of their great High Priest. Otherwise it will be impossible for them to exercise the faith which is essential *at this time or to occupy the position which God designs them to fill*" (*The Great Controversy,* p. 488, emphasis mine).

"At this time" and "position which God designs them to fill" is applicable only after the investigative judgment began in 1844.

Christ's "Essential" Ministry in the Judgment—Our Deliverer

We have already seen that one of the great things that happened in 1844 was the coming of the gift of prophecy in the writings of Ellen White as a messenger to the remnant church. What has she brought to our attention about Christ's work from the heavenly sanctuary and His second coming? Answer: a work that is necessary; a work that is essential! Essential for what? I propose that it is essential in order to give God the right to blot out the sins of the righteous and to destroy Satan, sin, and sinners, thus completing the atonement or the plan of salvation.

Remember that the plan of salvation is not completed until "the great controversy is ended. Sin and sinners are no more. The entire universe is clean. One pulse of harmony and gladness beats through the vast creation" (*The Great Controversy,* p. 678).

The statement above about Christ's intercession on man's behalf, being *"essential to the plan of salvation,"* is soon followed by:

> Through defects in the character, Satan works to gain control of the whole mind, and he knows that if these defects are cherished, he will succeed. Therefore he is constantly seeking to deceive the followers of Christ with his fatal sophistry that it is impossible for them to overcome. But Jesus pleads in their behalf His wounded hands, His bruised body; and He declares to all who would follow Him: 'My grace is sufficient for thee.'... Let none, then, regard their defects as incurable. God will give faith and grace to overcome them" (Ibid., p. 489).

It appears that Christ's *essential ministry* pictured here is not to plead with the Father but is to plead with us, declare to us, assure us, persuade us, and enable us to *overcome* our *defects of character*. When He says, "My grace is sufficient for you" (2 Cor. 12:9), He is not saying, "By My merits you are saved; you don't have to overcome anything." He is saying, "My grace will supply whatever you need to overcome." But the next question is, "Is overcoming something that would be *nice* to do or something that we *must* do by the last generation in order to complete the plan of salvation? There *is* something more to be done than simply being forgiven as indicated by the following:

> The forgiveness of sins is not the sole [only] result of the death of Jesus. He made the infinite

> sacrifice, not only that sin might be removed,
> but that human nature might be restored, re-
> beautified, reconstructed from its ruins, and
> made fit for the presence of God (*Testimonies
> for the Church,* vol. 5, p. 537).

"Made fit for the presence of God." Must this fitness for the presence of God, this restoration of human nature, be accomplished here and now before the last generation can go to heaven, or does that happen only after we get to heaven? It surely didn't happen to the thief on the cross. But the thief on the cross didn't have the time or the Spirit of Prophecy given to the remnant church. More, much more is expected of the last generation than of the thief on the cross. In fact, Christ cannot return until that restoration is completed.

> Christ is waiting with longing desire for the
> manifestation of Himself in His church. When
> the character of Christ shall be perfectly re-
> produced in His people, then He will come
> to claim them as His own (*Christ's Object Les-
> sons,* p. 69).

Notice the words "His church" and "His people." She is not talking about an isolated individual such as Enoch or Job but about a whole group of people who have learned to get along, people who have learned to love as Christ loved. "All the members are to draw together, that the church may become a spectacle to the world, to angels, and to men.... The church is to be as God designed it should be, a representative of God's family in another world" (*Selected Messages,* book 3, pp. 16, 17).

The following is how they are *enabled* to get along: "Those who accept Christ as their Saviour, becoming partakers of His divine nature, are enabled to follow His example, living in obedience to every precept of the law. Through the merits of Christ, man is to show by his obedience that he could be trusted in heaven, that he would not rebel" (*That I May Know Him,* p. 292).

Notice the words above, "partakers of His divine nature," and the words in the next quotation, "Christ has given His spirit as a divine power to overcome all hereditary and cultivated tendencies to evil, and to impress His own character upon His church.... The very image of God is to be reproduced in humanity. The honor of God, the honor of Christ, is involved in the perfection of the character of His people" (*The Desire of Ages,* p. 671).

Accomplishing all the above by the last generation is not optional, it is *essential to completing the plan of salvation*, and it is what makes Christ's ministry in the sanctuary above an *essential* ministry during the investigative judgment. Through Christ we will *overcome* "all hereditary and cultivated tendencies to evil." And He will impress "His own character upon His people" and manifest the "very image of God" in His people, thus showing that we can be trusted.

Fortunately, He does not leave us alone to struggle by ourselves, for He sends His angels to help us. When I present the judgment from Daniel 7, I find that most, if not all, in the audience see *people* standing before God to be judged in verse 10. But look more closely. "A thousand thousands ministered to Him; ten thousand times ten thousand stood before Him. The court was seated, and the books were opened."

The "thousand thousands" are angels helping Him, bringing Him records, sorting, filing, etc. But the "ten thousand times ten thousand" are *also* angels standing before Him. This group is awaiting orders to go help people on earth. If you think I'm making this up, read Revelation 5:11: "Then I looked, and I heard the voice of many angels around the throne, the living creatures; and the elders; and the number of them was *ten thousand times ten thousand, and thousands of thousands.*" The ten thousand times ten thousand are angels awaiting a command to fly swiftly to your side.

When describing the investigative judgment, Ellen White writes, "And holy angels as ministers and witnesses, in number 'ten thousand times ten thousand, and thousands of thousands,' attend this great tribunal" (*The Great Controversy,* p. 479). But there is more:

> He [Christ] is in His holy place, not in a state of solitude and grandeur, but *surrounded by ten thousand times ten thousand of heavenly beings* who wait to do their Master's bidding. And *He bids them go and work for the weakest saint who puts his trust in God. High and low, rich and poor, have the same help provided* (*SDA Bible Commentary,* vol. 7A, p. 481).

Remember, Daniel 7 convenes the investigative judgment that happened on the Day of Atonement. On that day only the high priest was to enter the sanctuary, no other human. Furthermore, the Day of Atonement was not one of the three annual feasts where all men came to Jerusalem. But the angels were there woven into the sanctuary curtains.

Looking to the heavenly sanctuary, the ministration of the angels to God's people on earth during the investigative judgment is possibly the most important half of the judgment—to teach, rule, deliver, and bring His people to perfection.

But why is the perfection of God's people essential? Hasn't Christ already obeyed perfectly and overcome for us? And why does this essentialness come to light now in these last days? Because, as stated above, Ellen White is not talking about individual salvation. That has already been accomplished by Jesus and given as a gift to each person who accepts Him. She is talking about a demonstration by the church that is essential to *completing* the plan of salvation. There is much at stake in the perfection of His people. "The honor of God, the honor of Christ, is involved in the perfection of the character of His people" (*The Desire of Ages,* p. 671).

Now if all these phrases, "perfection of the character of His people," "the very image of God is to be reproduced in His people," "overcome all hereditary and cultivated tendencies to evil," sound scary to you, and you are conditioned to think *sinless perfection* when you read them, which the Bible never requires, go back and read chapter 2 again. What the angels are waiting for is a group of people who are so committed to God and His law in a lawless world that they can be trusted in heaven not to rebel.

Man Is to Show, to Show, to Show

> Those who accept Christ as their Saviour, be-
> coming partakers of His divine nature, are en-
> abled to follow His example, living in obedi-
> ence to every precept of the law. Through the
> merits of Christ, *man is to show by his obedi-*
> *ence that he could be trusted in heaven, that he*
> *would not rebel* (*That I May Know Him*, p. 292,
> emphasis mine).

The backdrop stretched across this theater of the
universe is the law. Everything God does must be in
harmony with the moral law of the universe. That is why
we see legal terms appearing in the strangest places like,
"If we confess our sins, He is faithful and *just* to forgive
us our sins and to cleanse us from all unrighteousness" (1
John 1:9). Just? Yes, just! He has a legal right to forgive us.
But what has given Him that right to forgive the righteous
and to destroy the wicked so that the redeemed proclaim,
"*Just* and true are Your ways, O King of the saints!" (Rev.
15:3)? We turn now to an essential part of the work of
the atonement and of the investigative judgment, to that
which is essential to the deliverance of His people.

Christ was sinless. Jesus knew no sin. He was the
perfect image of God in moral character, disposition, and
attitude. He was a joy to be with. Every good person loved
him, loved to be with Him, and wanted to be close to Him.
You and I are to become like Him.

But there is a difference between Jesus and us. When
Jesus came into the world, He came in connected to the

Father via the Holy Spirit, who was in Him from birth, for He was fathered by the Holy Spirit. The angel Gabriel said to Mary, "The Holy Spirit will come upon you, and the power of the Highest will overshadow you; therefore, also, that Holy One who is to be born will be called the Son of God" (Luke 1:35).

> Christ came to the earth, taking humanity and standing as man's representative, to show in the controversy with Satan that man, *as God created him, connected with the Father and the Son,* could obey every divine requirement (*SDA Bible Commentary,* vol. 7, p. 926, emphasis mine).

> Christ is called the second Adam. In purity and holiness, connected with God and beloved by God, *He began where the first Adam began.* Willingly *He passed over the ground where Adam fell,* and redeemed Adam's failure (*SDA Bible Commentary,* vol. 7a, p. 446).

But you and I came into the world *disconnected.* When Adam and Eve were created, they were organically connected to God by His Holy Spirit. Consequently their natures were unselfish, pure, loving, and inclined naturally toward obedience. But when Adam, by deliberate choice, disobeyed God, that connection was broken. In their disconnected state, both Adam and Eve quickly became self-centered, self-protective, and inclined naturally toward disobedience. We saw the immediate effects and heard the hurtful words of Adam, "The woman whom You gave to be with me, she gave me of the tree, and I ate" (Gen. 3:12). Oh brother! How far he fell in just a few hours! He not only blamed his beautiful wife whom he had grown to adore so much that he chose her over God but then he blamed God too. And here he was in communion with God every day, and so soon after his creation! What hope do we, who are so far removed and degenerated from God's original creation, have to make wise choices? Fortunately, we have a lot going for us that Adam didn't if we will take advantage of it. But right now we are dealing with the essentiality of it.

Since the fall, every child of Adam comes into the world *disconnected* from God. That is what David meant when he said, "Behold, I was brought forth in iniquity, and in sin my mother conceived me" (Ps. 51:5). It's not a sin for married people to conceive. God said, "Be fruitful and multiply" (Gen. 1:28). Understand also that sin, sinfulness, and sinful nature is not a *thing* that is in us. It is the *lack* of something. It is the lack of a connection with God. Without that connection we are inclined naturally to sin. We are born with a propensity to sin. At some point by one's choice, we must be reconnected with the Holy Spirit, which we call being born again, new birth, or conversion.

In our disconnected state from birth, we develop evil brain nerve pathways of lying, cheating, self-preservation, selfishness, untrustworthiness, and moral weaknesses. You can see whole lists in Ephesians 5:3, 4 and Galatians 5:19-21.

But all those can be overcome. "Christ has given His spirit as a divine power to overcome all hereditary and cultivated tendencies to evil, and to impress His own character upon His church.... The very image of God is to be reproduced in humanity. The honor of God, the honor of Christ, is involved in the perfection of the character of His people" (*The Desire of Ages,* p. 671). And this perfecting of the character of His people is essential to the plan of salvation.

Since Jesus was born connected and we are not, you might be tempted to say, "Hey, that's not fair! Jesus had an advantage over us." Absolutely He did. But fix this forever in your sanctified mind: We are not in competition with Jesus! We cannot and never will be as pure as Jesus this side of the millennium. Jesus is your Savior. He takes His perfect righteousness and applies it to your account, so that when your name is called in the judgment, Jesus stands in your place. He and He alone is your Savior. You can never be as righteous as He this side of heaven, nor are you expected to be even when reconnected and the image of God is "perfectly" formed in you. The old nature is still there, and it will hound you for a little while even after your sins are blotted out.

When Jesus blots out your sins from the heavenly sanctuary, He not only blots them out of the record so they will not be seen in the great white throne panorama but He selectively eliminates those corrupt nerve pathways from your brain so that you cannot even remember having done them. That is wonderful grace in action. But we will still have a great sense of unworthiness as we wonder if there is anything we have not confessed and cleared that would embarrass our Lord and guardian angel. It's only when this mortal shall put on immortality, and this corruptible shall put on incorruption, that we will shed the old nature completely.

Even though Jesus inherited human nature and weaknesses from Mary after 4,000-plus years of degeneration since Creation, He never developed the evil brain nerve pathways we develop because He was connected to the Holy Spirit from birth. He never had to be "born again" or "converted." He had no evil propensities, inclinations to sin. But we do. Yes, I'm aware of the debate over the definition of *propensities*, so if you want to see what Ellen White meant when she used that term, see the appendix. If Jesus had come into the world disconnected, He would have been "brought forth in iniquity" and would have unavoidably committed all sorts of sins as we do and would have had to die for His own sins rather than being sinless and dying for *our* sins.

"Christ did not possess the same sinful, corrupt, fallen disloyaty we possess, for then he could not be a perfect offering. —Manuscript 94, 1893" (*Selected Messages,* book 3, p. 131).

Consider Hebrews 2:17, which says, "Therefore, in *all* things He had to be made like His brethren." "All," "every," or "none" seldom mean in Scripture what they usually mean to us today (see the appendix for examples). Jesus could not have been like everyone else in *all* things. One person varies from another in physical, mental, and emotional capacities, which affect our moral development. Nor could He have been made like us today because we have undergone another 2,000 years of degeneration since Jesus was here.

If because of the difference between Christ and you, you say, "That's not fair," you are not alone. You are expressing a haunting misconception held by many; the misconception that since Jesus is our example, we must be as good as He, which we can't be, so we subliminally resent Him and God. Please keep uppermost in your mind that you are not in competition with Jesus, and you can never be as sinless as He because you still have those awful brain nerve pathways developed by your past corrupt life. But the good news is that you can overcome them all, and you will if you are part of the final demonstration to the universe for which Christ is ministering in the sanctuary above, to show by our obedience that we can be trusted not to rebel in heaven. This is the position Christ wants us to fill now.

> The subject of the sanctuary and the investigative judgment should be clearly understood by the people of God. All need a knowledge for themselves of the position and work of their great High Priest. Otherwise it will be impossible for them to exercise the faith which is essential *at this time or to occupy the position which God designs them to fill* (*The Great Controversy,* p. 488, emphasis mine).

We have a part to play in the plan of salvation, and it's not an easy part. In fact, it is a rather demanding part. We are to overcome every inherited and every cultivated defect of character, and we cannot, we absolutely cannot, do that if we are refusing to follow the many health counsels the Lord has graciously given to us, His remnant people. "It is impossible for men and women, with all their sinful, health-destroying, brain-enervating habits, to discern sacred truth, through which they are to be sanctified, refined, elevated, and made fit for the society of heavenly angels in the kingdom of glory" (*Counsels on Diet and Foods,* p. 70).

Angels Want to Know

Satan's accusations are that human beings are a defective creation who cannot obey God's law; therefore, they should be annihilated. Jesus proved that a human being, when connected to God, *can* obey God's law. Jesus' relationship with His heavenly Father was a testimony to heaven of a beautiful, loving life—a life in full surrender and obedience to God.

But the question that remains is, can human beings who are *disconnected* at birth, who have developed sinful nerve pathways etched deeply into their giant boutons, who have lived a corrupt life and are then connected to God, can these corrupted human beings be restored to the image of God where they are safe to save? It seems to me that this is what has yet to be shown.

The righteous angels remember what heaven was like before sin arose. They are working tirelessly to restore that again. They *will* not, they *cannot*, tolerate rebellion in heaven again. So they must have more evidence to refute Satan's accusations that humans are a defective creation. They cannot be satisfied with Christ's perfection alone because He came into the world connected. If the plan of restoration depended alone on Christ's righteous life, we could have gone home a thousand years ago,.

Nor can the angels be satisfied with an isolated case here and there. They need to see a large group of re-connected people able to get along. For if the following has kept us in the world -- "It is the unbelief, the worldliness, unconsecration, and strife among the Lord's professed people that have kept us in this world of sin and sorrow so many years," then it seems to me that if God's people were to overcome their "unbelief, ... worldliness, unconsecration, and strife" with each other, we wouldn't have to stay here any longer. The "work" of spreading the everlasting gospel and purifying the church would finish in a hurry.

Furthermore, the angels need to see God's people getting along in a *sinful* world. If they can see us getting along in a *sinful* world, they will believe that it can happen in a *sinless* world. The millions who have not had the benefit of the light given to the remnant, but who have lived up to the light they had at the time, can be and will be perfected in the sinless world of heaven and the new earth where there will be no tempter. But the angels need to see it here.

That's why we read, "Through the merits of Christ, man is to show by his obedience that he could be trusted in heaven, that he would not rebel" (*That I May Know Him*, p. 292).

From time to time I have seen this love and obedience at work among God's working believers fulfilling Ellen White's statement, "When men are bound together, not by force or self-interest, but by love, they show the working of an influence that is above every human influence. Where this oneness exists, it is evidence that the image of God is being restored in humanity, that a new principle of life has been implanted. It shows that there is power in the divine nature to withstand the supernatural agencies of evil, and that the grace of God subdues the selfishness inherent in the natural heart" (*The Desire of Ages,* p. 678). This is wonderful to behold! This is wonderful to experience!

God took great risks in creating humans with the power of choice. They chose wrongly. God then stuck His neck out for His creation. He put Himself on the line in behalf of the human race. He has altered the Godhead for all eternity in order to save this fallen race. Unfathomable grace! Indescribable love! He took a risk in allowing His Son to become a human. He even ran the risk of taking a few to heaven before the price for their redemption was paid—He took Enoch and Moses and Elijah to heaven before Jesus died for them, before the bill had been paid. They were saved on credit. All because He loves us!

I know this can be a provocative statement, but in a sense, God does not have the right to forgive man his confessed sins until He has proven that His plan of restoration works. And that plan is to be proven by the last generation, the faithful remnant, "who keep the commandments of God and have the testimony of Jesus Christ" (Rev. 12:17).

Likewise, God does not have the legal right to forgive the millions past, counting them restored, until after he has proof that humanity can be restored. In my opinion, "the intercession of Christ in man's behalf in the sanctuary above is as essential to the plan of salvation as His death on the cross" (*The Great Controversy,* p. 489). God works on faith in what will be accomplished. And God is waiting with longing desire for His vindication to save us. The ball is in our court.

The Honor of God, the Honor of Christ

So the investigative judgment is not yet completed, not until a demonstration is made. "Man is to *show* by his obedience that he could be trusted in heaven" (*The Faith I Live By,* p. 114). "Christ is waiting with longing desire for the manifestation of Himself in His church. When the character of Christ shall be perfectly produced in His people, then He will come to claim them as his own" (*Christ's Object Lessons,* p. 69). "The very image of God is to be reproduced in humanity. The honor of God, the honor of Christ, is involved in the perfection of the character of His people" (*The Desire of Ages,* p. 671).

When that demonstration is completed to the satisfaction of the angels, Satan's accusations will have been proven false. The annihilation of the human race he demanded will fall back on him and his followers. Human beings are not a defective creation when connected to God. God now has the justification needed to punish the wicked. Remember that the annihilation of the wicked is an act of mercy to everyone. When the Spirit of God is withdrawn from the earth, words cannot describe the horror, the dread, the darkness—not one of Satan's followers will be safe. Men will wish for death to escape the dreadful suffering. So God will grant them their wish.

God has waited a very long time to bring this drama to

a close. In performing His work as a biblical judge during the investigative judgment, Christ has gifted us from the holy of holies with the Spirit of Prophecy writings to *teach* us, to beneficently call us back to the Bible to *rule* us, to *deliver* us from the corruption of a wicked world, and to enable His people to show the universes that God's human creation can be trusted not to rebel in heaven or to defile heaven. This demonstration is an *essential ministry*— essential to show to the angels, essential to complete the plan of salvation. Are you willing to be part of that demonstration? Are you willing to be delivered from all the evil in the world? Are you yearning to be judged?

Chapter 9

The Sanctuary Justified

This chapter sets forth, in outline form with references, but not always quotes, a study of the sanctuary. I will first support the traditional Adventist interpretation, then suggest an alternative reading of Daniel 8:14 that fits the interpretation I'm suggesting of the investigative judgment better than the standard reading from the King James Version.

The Millerite message was built on Daniel 8:14: "then the sanctuary shall be cleansed." William Miller and his followers believed that Jesus was coming in 1843, then 1844 to cleanse the earth. William Miller's message was built on two errors; the common belief that:

1. The sanctuary of Daniel 8:14 was this earth instead of the heavenly sanctuary.
2. The earth (the sanctuary) would be cleansed at Christ's second coming rather than at the end of the millennium.

Seventh-day Adventists have built an elaborate theology on the "cleansing of the heavenly sanctuary." I hasten to add that the doctrine of the heavenly sanctuary and its cleansing is not a rationalization to explain away the great disappointment of 1844. It is real, and it is true.

1. There *is* a heavenly sanctuary. "We have such a High Priest ... a Minister of the sanctuary and of the true tabernacle which the Lord erected, and not man" (Heb. 8:1, 2).
2. The heavenly sanctuary needs cleansing. "And according to the law almost all things are purified [*cleansed*] with blood, and without shedding of blood there is no remission [*forgiveness*]. Therefore it was necessary that the copies of the things in the heavens should be *purified* [*cleansed*] with these, but *the heavenly things* themselves [*purified, cleansed*] with better sacrifices than these" (Heb. 9:22, 23, emphasis mine).
3. The earthly sanctuary and priesthood were symbols of the true or heavenly sanctuary: "who serve the copy and shadow of the heavenly things" (Heb. 8:5).
4. The ceremonies of the earthly sanctuary symbolized God's plan of restoration.
   a. "I was envious of the boastful, when I saw the prosperity of the wicked.... Until I went into the sanctuary of God; Then I understood their end" (Ps. 73:3, 17).
   b. I use the term "plan of restoration" here instead of plan of salvation or plan of redemption because the latter two are often limited in our minds to Christ's death on the cross and our acceptance of it as our means of salvation. That's true, but God's plan of salvation or redemption is not limited to the

cross. It comprehends even more than Eden to Eden, i.e. the fall of man, for it reaches back to include the apostasy of Lucifer and stretches forward to his elimination. So the plan of salvation is His plan of restoration, which is not completed until sin and sinners are no more and there is oneness throughout the universe for all eternity to come.

c. The plan of restoration carried out on earth is directed from the heavenly sanctuary. After the book of Hebrews places Christ in the heavenly sanctuary, it then shows that His work is here on earth, for the exhortation is, "If you endure chastening, God deals with you as with sons; for what son is there whom a father does not chasten?" (Heb. 12:7). That chastening proceeds from God from within the heavenly sanctuary where the Trinity is working to deliver and perfect their people on earth, especially during this antitypical day of atonement. I don't mean to confine either the Father or Jesus or the Holy Spirit to the sanctuary. They are all working down here. I am simply using sanctuary language to make a point. Most of the events depicted in the book of Revelation proceed by God's directions from the heavenly sanctuary. Remember how He gave us great light on earth every time He made a major move in the heavenly sanctuary.

d. The complete and completed plan of restoration was especially symbolized by the annual ceremonies: Passover, Feast of Weeks, Day of Atonement and Feast of Tabernacles. These ceremonies unveiled God's plan of restoration. They also are a prediction of the fulfillment of His plan of restoration.

5. The earthly sanctuary was cleansed once a year on the Day of Atonement. The annual ceremonies—Passover, Pentecost, Day of Atonement, Feast of Tabernacles—were spread out throughout a one-year cycle and were repeated year after year as God had instructed. While the earthly Day of Atonement ceremony took one day to complete, the antitypical Day of Atonement takes many years—from 1844 until after the millennium with the destruction of Satan and his followers.

a. On the Day of Atonement the *sanctuary proper was cleansed* from the uncleanness (the sins, the contamination) of the children of Israel, and *the people themselves were cleansed* from all their sins before the Lord. The terms "making an atonement" and "cleansing from sin" mean virtually the same thing and can be used interchangeably:

i. "So he shall *make atonement* for the Holy Place, because of the uncleanness of the children of Israel, and because of their transgressions, for all their sins; and so he shall do for the tabernacle of meeting which remains among them in the midst of their uncleanness" (Lev. 16:16).

ii. "Then he shall sprinkle some of the blood on it with his finger seven times, *cleanse it*, and consecrate it from the uncleanness of the children of Israel" (verse 19). Notice how *"make atonement"* and *"cleanse"* are parallel, meaning the same thing. As a matter of polemic interest, one could even say that the atonement is made by the cleansing, for atonement is made by the high priest sprinkling the blood seven times. That took more than a moment. The atonement is not completed in a day, not until the people and the heavens and earth are cleansed.

iii. On the same day *repentant people* were also cleansed. "For on that day the priest shall *make atonement* for you, to *cleanse* you, that you may be clean from all your sins before the LORD" (verse 30).

"Then he shall make atonement for the Holy Sanctuary, and he shall make atonement for the tabernacle of meeting and for the altar, and he shall make atonement *for the priests and for all the people* of the assembly. This shall be an everlasting statute for you, to make atonement for the children of Israel, for all their sins, once a year" (verses 33, 34).

b. During the solemn Day of Atonement, the people were to do a special work of putting sin out of their lives. "In the seventh month, on the tenth day of the month, you shall afflict your souls [humble yourselves]" (verse 29).

Atonement for an individual can be seen in three parts. First, Christ's sinless life and death is the atoning sacrifice. Second, when we accept Christ as our Savior, His perfect life is placed to our account so that we are treated as He deserves. Then comes part three, the cleansing of the sanctuary *and* the people. Atonement is not finished when Christ applies His righteousness to our account because atonement includes both cleansing the record and cleansing the person, just as it includes cleansing heaven and earth.

Cleansing His followers involves an *active* role by the people, a *cooperative* role by the people in being cleansed of their sins since only those persons who had confessed their sins were forgiven and had atonement made for them. And add to that, that confession of sin is of no value unless the person repents, turns from the sin, and tries to live righteously. Atonement is more than a judicial pronouncement in which only the *record* of the people's sins is cleansed without any concurrent purification of the people. Atonement is a cleansing of the record *and* a cleansing of the people. When we speak of a cleansing of the people, it is worth noting that absolute sinlessness is not to be expected before we are glorified at Christ's second coming, but we can resist the evil tendencies, those evil propensities that lead us into sin.

"We are now living in the great day of atonement. In the typical service, while the high priest was making the atonement for Israel, all were required to afflict their souls by repentance of sin and humiliation before the Lord, lest they be cut off from among the people. In like manner, all who would have their names retained in the book of life should now, in the few remaining days of their probation, afflict their souls before God by sorrow for sin and true repentance. There must be deep, faithful searching of heart. The light, frivolous spirit indulged by so many professed Christians must be put away. There is earnest warfare before all who would subdue the evil tendencies that strive for the mastery. The work of preparation is an individual work. We are not saved in groups. The purity and devotion of one will not offset the want of these qualities in another. Though all nations are to pass in judgment before God, yet He will examine the case of each individual with as close and searching scrutiny as if there were not another being upon the earth. Everyone must be tested and found without spot or wrinkle or any such thing" (*The Great Controversy,* pp. 489, 490).

i.   Even though the morning and evening sacrifices and the annual ceremonial feasts were repeated again and again over the years, these ceremonies represented in real time only *one* plan of salvation (Heb. 9:25, 26). So just as Christ was crucified *once*, so the heavenly sanctuary is cleansed but *once,* and the people are cleansed only *once* in God's plan of redemption, but that cleansing takes several years to accomplish. There is no "second chance" after death. The truth is that we have hundreds of chances in this life to repent of our sins.

ii. The Day of Atonement came near the end of the year as the last ceremony before the Feast of Tabernacles, the latter representing our eternal home in the new heaven and new earth. Therefore, the antitypical day of atonement happens shortly before the second coming of Christ when we go to heaven to celebrate the antitypical feast of tabernacles.

iii. The ceremonial Day of Atonement was more than symbolic. It was a real day of judgment to those living at that time, yet it also symbolized the final day of judgment consisting of three phases: 1) the investigative phase that is taking place now, which includes blotting out the sins of the righteous and transferring them to the head of Satan who is sent into the wilderness for 1,000 years; 2) the "appeal" or the review by the righteous of the sentences upon the wicked during the millennium; and 3) the executive judgment or execution of the wicked. This is the *end* of sin. So, the antitypical day of atonement takes more than 1,000 years in real time—the first phase, the investigative part, then the work of review by the saints while Satan and his angels are in the wilderness of a demolished earth for 1,000 years, then the executive part where Satan and his followers are executed, and then follows the new heaven and new earth.

The Adventist doctrine of cleansing the sanctuary and the people is well supported in Scripture and, of course, the writings of Ellen White.

However, while the authorized version and the New King James Version follow the Septuagint for Daniel 8:14, which translates *sadaq* as *katharisthesetai,* "then shall the sanctuary be *cleansed,*" the majority of Bibles translate from the Hebrew, "Then shall the sanctuary be *justified*" for *sadaq.* Review the following versions:

- "then the holy place will be properly restored" (NASB)
- "then the sanctuary will be reconsecrated" (NIV)
- "then the sanctuary will have its rights restored" (JB)

- "then the rights of the sanctuary will be restored" (MLB)
- "then the sanctuary shall be restored to its rightful state" (RSV)

The *SDA Bible Commentary* lists the following words as interpretations to the text: "be righted," "be put right," "be put in a rightful condition," "be justified," "be vindicated."

As Adventists we have been criticized for building our doctrine of *cleansing* the sanctuary on the King James Version instead of from the Hebrew. The truth is that while "cleansed" is acceptable based on what actually happened on the Day of Atonement, translating the Hebrew *sadaq* as *justified* or *vindicated* or *be restored to its rightful state* may fit our doctrine of the sanctuary even better: "then shall the sanctuary be justified" or "restored" or "vindicated."

Vindicating the Sanctuary

One thing I have not discussed is how Roman Catholic theology ignores and replaces the heavenly sanctuary with its priests, its church, and Mary as the means of salvation and intercession. The sanctuary truth needs to be restored. Adventist theology restores the sanctuary to its rightful state giving the sanctuary its rights. Redundancy intended!

Also, as mentioned earlier, the earthly sanctuary not only unveils God's plan of restoration but it predicts events that will happen. As those predictions are fulfilled, the sanctuary ministry is proven to be true. It is "vindicated" and "restored" to its rightful status in our understanding.

In a way, the earthly sanctuary services began with Adam after his fall because we see him offering his sacrifices, showing his need for and faith in a vicarious atonement. The sanctuary services were formalized and expanded when the earthly sanctuary in the wilderness was built. And the vicarious atonement was ultimately provided by the unblemished, perfect sacrifice of Christ. Christ showed that humans when connected to God from birth were not a defective creation. Christ's perfect fulfillment of the law earned Him the right to redeem and cleanse His followers, which He does by reconnecting them to the Holy Spirit, giving them a new nature along with supernatural strength to overcome sin. *The believer is cleansed as evil tendencies are eradicated out of his life.* That should be obvious. As long as a sin is cherished and practiced, a person is not cleansed.

So I am suggesting that something more is needed to justify the sanctuary and complete the plan of restoration. Christ's perfect fulfillment of the law made legitimate the rest of the plan of reconciliation. But the jury is still out. One more condition must be met before peace will be permanently restored—the perfecting of the saints in order to justify God's right to cleanse heaven. Cleansing heaven includes destroying the accuser of the brethren, Satan, who claims that human beings are a defective creation who cannot obey God's law and should therefore be eradicated. That claim must be proven wrong. It is by perfecting once-disconnected saints who are now connected that his claim is proven groundless, which gives God the right to destroy evil. Christ came into the world connected to God via the Holy Spirit. He was never carnal. We come into the world disconnected and corrupt in mind. After we are connected to God at conversion, by His strengthening grace we are now enabled to live obediently, "that the righteous requirement of the law might be fulfilled in us who do not walk according to the flesh but according to the Spirit" (Rom. 8:4), thereby demonstrating that human beings are safe to save.

The various animal sacrifices met their predictive fulfillment in Christ's perfect life and substitutionary death. But there was more predicted in the sanctuary services than the death of Christ. The cleansing of the sanctuary symbolized the cleansing of His people and the universe. It is clear to see that the cleansing of the universe involves the active eradication of Satan and his followers. That is no paper transaction. It should likewise be clear that the cleansing of God's people is not just a judicial paper transaction but an active eradication of evil from the believer's life.

The restoration of once disconnected saints to a heavenly righteousness is the ultimate accomplishment of the heavenly sanctuary ministry. Such righteousness has been seen here and there in isolated individuals in generations past, but the last generation is to manifest that level of righteousness on a larger scale while living here on earth. *That* demonstration by the remnant church becomes the sanctuary's vindication that God's plan of restoration works. It does what it was intended to do. If that level of righteousness can happen in reconnected persons living here on a sinful earth amidst Satan's fiercest temptations, then it can happen for all the redeemed who died short of that righteousness who will be raised to live in a sinless heaven and on a sinless earth with no tempter around.

The sanctuary is not vindicated, justified, or restored to its rightful place until its primary purpose is accomplished, and its primary purpose is the restoration of the image of Christ in every believer, which is accomplished during and by all that transpires under the term the investigative judgment—teaching, ruling, delivering, deciding—and a little more during the time of Jacob's trouble.

Christ came into the world connected to God with no propensities to sin, and He lived a perfect life. All Adam's offspring come into the world disconnected from God with propensities to sin, and we develop those propensities even further. The purpose of God's plan of restoration is to restore man where he will never sin again. The sanctuary services illustrate God's plan of restoration. If the restoration fails, it shows that the sanctuary services were flawed, but if the restoration succeeds, then the sanctuary and all its truths are vindicated. The vindication of the sanctuary, "then shall the sanctuary be restored to its rightful place" (Dan. 8:14, RSV), depends upon the restoration of man to the image of Christ.

Man was created with free will and freedom of choice. God does not know, cannot know, beforehand the choices we will make. He took a chance in sending Jesus that He might fail. He is taking a chance that reconnected human beings might fail. In the sanctuary services He has put His investment in the human race on display. He has put His judgment, His evaluation of our worth at risk.

The sanctuary services reveal God's love, His investment in humanity via the eternal incarnation, His risk-taking, and the value He places on His human creation, unworthy as we may appear. If His plan is successful, it vindicates His investment, and thereby vindicates the earthly sanctuary, which typified it, and the heavenly sanctuary, which administers it. The first part, Christ's life on earth was successful. Now the last part, the purification of God's remnant people is in process.

Are we a help or a hindrance to His sanctuary?

Chapter 10

Summary

Some Adventists have lost faith in Ellen White, in the sanctuary doctrine, and in the investigative judgment due, in my opinion, to their limited understanding of the investigative judgment. The chapter in the book *The Great Controversy* titled "The Investigative Judgment" pictures Christ going over the records of professed saints to see who will be saved and who will not. But the investigative judgment and the day of atonement involves more than what is pictured in that one chapter. It involves the rest of the book, including the whole process of Christ delivering His people from the evils of this world beginning in 1844, to the elimination of evil completely.

The judgment hour message of Revelation 14 proclaims the investigative judgment as part of the everlasting gospel which is "good news" because, as a result of that judgment, the lost dominion (kingdom) is taken from the little horn and given to the saints of the Most High. A biblical judge does more than a U.S. judge who sits behind a bench. A biblical judge rules, teaches, decides, and delivers. Therefore, as a biblical judge, Christ is actively ruling His people, teaching them, and delivering them from evil even now. The righteous want to be delivered, judged. They need not fear the judgment. Christ and the Father are on their side deciding in their favor.

To assure His people that the investigative judgment began in 1844, that same year Christ gave a phenomenal spiritual gift to the remnant church in the life and ministry of Ellen G. White. The presence of this phenomenon in the Adventist church is tangible evidence that Christ did in fact enter the Most Holy Place of the heavenly sanctuary in 1844 to complete the atonement. And that gift is one of the very ways Christ is "judging" His church, i.e. is teaching us, ruling us, delivering us, and directing us to the Bible as the final authority by which our lives are blessed and measured.

The Day of Atonement ceremony in the earthly sanctuary made clear that the atonement is not completed until sin and sinners are destroyed. By what right can God destroy Satan and his followers? Satan charged that God's law cannot be obeyed and, therefore, should be annihilated. But Christ's perfect life disproved that charge. Yet more is needed. The annual cleansing of the earthly sanctuary and the cleansing of God's people symbolized the perfecting of His people, which is an essential part of the atonement. Restoring the image of God in once-carnal people is needed to give God the right to destroy sinners and forgive saints.

Angels, who lived in the pure atmosphere of heaven before sin arose, never want sin to enter heaven again. Christ's life showed that human beings who are connected to the Father can live above sin. But there is a difference between Christ and the rest of humanity. Christ came into the world connected to the Holy Spirit. He was fathered by the Holy Spirit. Jesus was sinless from birth. He did not need to be converted or reconnected as we do. Therefore, His perfection does not quite satisfy the angels. They need to see if humans, who have come into the world disconnected from God and corrupted by sin, who are then reconnected to the Holy Spirit, can live a perfect life in a sinful world. That demonstration will be seen in the last generation, the 144,000. Then the angels will know that believers who, through the ages, died short of becoming perfect can reach perfection in a perfect world where there is no tempter.

While none can be as sinless as Christ this side of heaven, they can be considered righteous by their undeviating commitment to Christ. Such a commitment will eventually lead to willing obedience to all God's laws. Biblical "perfection" is unswerving allegiance to God more than it is absolute sinlessness. It is possible to believe that God accounts us righteous because of Christ's imputed and imparted righteousness even in the face of our guilty feelings, which we must lay at the foot of the cross.

God's way is in the sanctuary. The earthly sanctuary services depicted God's plan of restoration directed from the heavenly sanctuary. But the heavenly sanctuary ministry was virtually eclipsed by the little horn. If the three angels' messages containing the sanctuary truth are successful at cleansing His people and restoring His image in His church, then Christ will have proven that His restoration plan worked, which restores the sanctuary to its rightful place in the eyes of all. It justifies the sanctuary.

As we close this book, remember that the Bible is real. The gift of prophecy in the writings of Ellen White is real. The heavenly sanctuary is real. The investigative judgment beginning in 1844 is real. The ministry of Christ emanating from the Most Holy Place is real and in process now to perfect a people ready for translation. It is an essential ministry to justify the sanctuary, to complete the atonement, and to demonstrate to all heaven that human beings can be a trustworthy part of a harmonious universe. All the above is the purpose of and included in what is called the investigative judgment.

Appendix

Within the appendix, I want to draw attention to biblical and Spirit of Prophecy evidence in regards to use of the words "all," "none," and "every" in Scripture and the theme of propensity/propensities.

All, None, Every

Following are textual evidence that words like "all," "none," "every," etc. should not always be understood in their absolute sense. There are many more, but these serve to illustrate the common language used by Bible writers. We do the same today, like "I've told you a million times not to exaggerate."

- "Moreover, brethren, I do not want you to be unaware that all our fathers were under the cloud, all passed through the sea" (1 Cor. 10:1). Abraham, Isaac, Jacob, and even David are considered "fathers," yet they were not under the cloud nor passed through the sea. So the intent of this verse is that all the children of Israel who were there "were under the cloud."
- "He came to His own and His own did not receive

Him. But as many as received Him" (John 1:11, 12).

- "...and no one receives His testimony, He who has received His testimony..." (John 3:32, 33).
- "Then all the land of Judea, and those from Jerusalem, went out to him [John the Baptist] and were all baptized by him in the Jordan River, confessing their sins" (Mark 1:5). Many, yes, but not all.
- "But if we say, 'From men'—they feared the people, for all counted John to have been a prophet indeed" (Mark 11:32). Many, yes, but not all because "the Pharisees and lawyers rejected the will of God for themselves, not having been baptized by him" (Luke 7:30).
- "But those things which God foretold by the mouth of all His prophets, that the Christ would suffer, He has thus fulfilled" (Acts 3:18). Only some of the prophets predicted the suffering of the Messiah.
- "There is none righteous, no, not one" (Rom. 3:10), but Luke 1:6 says of Zacharias and his wife, "they were both righteous before God."

Propensity, Propensities

The following quotes are taken from the writings of Ellen White on the subject of our propensity to sin and Christ's sinless life.

- "He could have sinned; He could have fallen, but not for one moment was there in Him an evil propensity" (*The Faith I Live By,* p. 49).

- "God made Adam after His own character, pure and upright. There were no corrupt principles in the first Adam, no corrupt propensities or tendencies to evil. Adam was as faultless as the angels before God's throne" (*God's Amazing Grace,* p. 344).

- "Children are born with the animal propensities largely developed, the parents' own stamp of character having been given to them.... Children born to parents will almost invariably take naturally to the disgusting habits of secret vice.... The sins of the parents will be visited upon their children, because the parents have given them the stamp of their own lustful propensities" (*Child Guidance,* p. 442).

- "Without the transforming process which can come alone through divine power, the original propensities to sin are left in the heart in all their strength, to forge new chains, to impose a slavery that can never be broken by human power" (*Evangelism,* p. 192).

- "By every wholehearted, earnest sacrifice for the Master's service our powers will increase. While we yield ourselves as instruments for the Holy Spirit's working, the grace of God works in us to deny old inclinations, to overcome powerful propensities, and to form new habits. As we cherish and obey the promptings of the Spirit, our hearts are enlarged to receive more and more of His power, and to do more and better work" (*Christ's Object Lessons,* p.

354).

- "We need not retain one sinful propensity.... As we partake of the divine nature, hereditary and cultivated tendencies to wrong are cut away from the character, and we are made a living power for good. Ever learning of the divine Teacher, daily partaking of His nature, we cooperate with God in overcoming Satan's temptations" (*The Faith I Live By,* p. 23).

- "Christ ... is waiting to quicken your spiritual pulse to increased activity. No longer let any evil influence or propensity, natural or acquired, lead you to subordinate the claims of future, eternal interests to the common affairs of this life. No man can serve two masters..." (*The Upward Look,* p. 313).

- "Be careful, exceedingly careful as to how you dwell upon the human nature of Christ. Do not set Him before the people as a man with the propensities of sin. He is the second Adam. The first Adam was created a pure, sinless being, without a taint of sin upon him; he was in the image of God. He could fall, and he did fall through transgressing. Because of sin his posterity was born with inherent propensities of disobedience. But Jesus Christ was the only begotten Son of God. He took upon Himself human nature, and was tempted in all points as human nature is tempted. He could have sinned; He could have fallen, but not for one moment was there in Him an evil propensity. He was assailed with temptations in the wilderness, as Adam was assailed with temptations in Eden" (*SDA Bible Commentary,* vol. 5, p. 1128).

- "Christ is called the second Adam. In purity and holiness, connected with God and beloved by God, he began where the first Adam began" (*The Youth's Instructor,* June 2, 1898).

We invite you to view the complete
selection of titles we publish at:

www.TEACHServices.com

Please write or email us your praises, reactions, or
thoughts about this or any other book we publish at:

TEACH Services, Inc.
P U B L I S H I N G
www.TEACHServices.com

P.O. Box 954
Ringgold, GA 30736

info@TEACHServices.com

TEACH Services, Inc., titles may be purchased in bulk for
educational, business, fund-raising, or sales promotional use.
For information, please e-mail

BulkSales@TEACHServices.com

Finally, if you are interested in seeing
your own book in print, please contact us at

publishing@teachservices.com

We would be happy to review your manuscript for free.

www.ingramcontent.com/pod-product-compliance
Lightning Source LLC
Chambersburg PA
CBHW060540100426
42742CB00013B/2406